Simply Angelic

Divine Images

by
Tom and Carol Lumbrazo

Paulette

Blessings from the Church

Love

Tom Lumbrazo & Carol

Simply Angelic
Divine Images

by Tom and Carol Lumbrazo

Printed in China

Published by
When Angels Touch Publishing
1911 Douglas Boulevard # 85-140
Roseville, California 95661
916.782.8408

To order, go to www.whenangelstouch.com
or email Tom@whenangelstouch.com

ISBN: 978-0-615-79386-3

Wings of Angels

We have picked this cloud photograph as a representation of what this book is about – Angels and Angelic Beings in the form of clouds.

One afternoon, Tom took this photograph when this cloud came over his house. Not only did it appear to be very angelic with its wings, but it was so huge in the sky. It covered one-half of the visible sky. When Tom loaded the photo into his computer, there was no question what it was, and that it was so special. As you look at it, you can see it represents angel wings and notice the right wing is bent to imitate angel wings like you might see in books and paintings of angels. So Tom and Carol picked this very special photograph as the cover of this unique book of clouds and cloud messages.

So literally, on the "Wings of Angels," this book of Divine angelic cloud images, is brought to you...not only by Tom and Carol...but by the Creator above.

Dedication

This book is dedicated to the young children of our two nephews: Kaili, Zackery, Zoey, and Seamus; and to our friend Louis' daughter Tirza. It is our hope that these five children and others like them will help transform the Earth into a loving and caring place for all its inhabitants. The Earth must evolve into a place of positive energies, rather than the negative energies of hate, greed, jealousy, violence, and ego. Our children are the ones that can start now to make this happen through their own inner peace, love and leadership.

This book is also dedicated to the very special family members who passed in 2011 and 2012. Fern and John, Tom's parents, died in the summer of 2011. Carol's dad, Harold "Mac," died in the summer of 2012, and her aunt Glenola, died in the summer of 2011. Many of the thoughts in this book were taught to us by their loving guidance. Tom and Carol know that the love from these family members is still with them and continues to guide them every day.

About the Authors

Tom Lumbrazo is an author, photographer, planner, and artist. Tom has a background in government and spent 40 years as a City Planner and Planning Consultant in the Sacramento, California region. Tom can be described as a practical person who uses his five senses to evaluate any situation. In 2001, he had a near-death experience during a major car accident. Seconds before the accident, a strong male voice called out and directed him to slow from 60 mph to 35mph. Tom listened to this guidance immediately, and by going 35mph, his life was saved. Since that accident, his life has changed dramatically, leading him into the fields of photography, art, and writing. Along with this change in life interests, Tom has also gained the ability to see images and messages in such places as clouds, the natural landscape and trees, rocks, and sidewalks as well as in a paranormal sense.

Carol Lumbrazo spent her career working in libraries. Since childhood, books and reading have always been a significant part of her life. Travel is also one of her interests in life. Travel described in the stories and photos in this book has been like a dream come true for her. Changes in her life over the last few years, and Tom's new interests, have given her a new perspective on life and many new interests to explore and follow.

How to contact the authors...

By email:
Tom@whenangelstouch.com, or Carol@whenangelstouch.com

By mail:
When Angels Touch LLC
1191 Douglas Boulevard # 85-140
Roseville, CA 95661
Phone: 916.782.8408

Website: Whenangelstouch.com
and When Angels Touch Facebook

Table of Contents

Relevance and Purpose

During the last several years, Tom and Carol have come to understand that there is life in many forms living with all of us on and within our planet. On the personal side of this revelation is the fact that we humans are made up of millions of living things such as bacteria, which are necessary for us to function every day.

Some of the life we have encountered is unseen but living along side of us. Fortunately, Tom and Carol have been able to capture many of these invisible beings due to the technology of our modern cameras. This fact has opened their minds to the wholeness of life on this planet, and the interdependence of these various living beings.

As Tom and Carol followed their "path" and the guidance from many sources, they found that clouds were "talking" to them. This process started in 2007 when they traveled to Peru and Machu Picchu and saw the clouds of the Condor and Puma, two of the sacred entities of the Inca. Once they saw these amazing clouds, they could not stop looking upwards every day. As they did, more clouds were presented to them. So many, that they prepared two books to show these images. *Journey to the Clouds* was published in 2009 and *Faces of the Universe* in 2010. *Simply Angelic* is the third in their series of cloud books.

Tom and Carol have prepared this book to educate, to enlighten, and to share images in such unlikely places as clouds that are messages to all of us. This book is also intended to serve as a book of meditations. We hope your life is blessed with a desire to see the unseen and to speculate what all this may mean relative to our very existence. By discovering such images as shown in this book, Tom and Carol have found great feelings of love, joy, wonder, and generosity. Earth is the home to all of us. The Earth has simplicity and complexity at the same time. It is so magnificent and amazing to contemplate. Hopefully the human race is wise enough to serve and give back to this incredible place for future generations. Most of all, Tom and Carol want to convey a message of Love. For it is true that the most important thing is Love. There are all kinds of love. There is love in an unconditional sense, but more importantly, there is love of the divine.

Divine love is the love of all things that have been created by whatever Creator you believe in. The only truth is to honor that Divine Creation.

Tom and Carol feel that the clouds have an intelligence and that they are communicating to us, if we would only take the time to look and listen. The message is of Divine Love, and Love for our planet and to honor all life, including the planet itself as an entity. Unfortunately, there are many forces that are causing havoc and destruction of our natural environment and so we all have a lot of work to do to keep the planet in balance and to preserve its many inhabitants. Tom and Carol hope the cloud images in this book help you to appreciate all that we have, the many beings that are integral to the planet, and the importance of giving back to the planet Earth each day.

Acknowledgements

Creator/God/A Great Spirit

It is important to honor the Creator of all things. Whatever creator you believe in, it is manifested in our very existence and the meaning of our lives. When you see images as presented in this book, it could not have happened without the Creator. Tom and Carol find clouds to be especially beautiful and they function to allow all life on this planet.

Many people throughout the world have been or are experiencing what might be called a "spiritual transformation." Many, like Tom, have experienced this transformation after a near-death experience. And many of these people have written accounts or books on their transformation and what it might mean for others.

With this book, Tom and Carol have written three books on the subject of Cloud Messages. Tom feels he is very blessed to be able to find and take photographs of these incredible and amazing cloud images and to share them with you. Tom feels that these incredibly visual images help to document the spiritual changes he has experienced and talked about. Tom hopes that his work will help others to understand the Divine Nature of the world and that the sky does not have clouds just for rain, but for messages that all of us can experience.

Psychic Friends

Many of Tom and Carol's friends are blessed with incredible intuitive talents. Carol and Tom have found them to be gifted, wise, giving, and loving. Without their guidance, their adventures since 2001 could never have happened. A special thanks goes to all of them including Alan, Amanda, Emerald, Francie Marie, Judith, Kathleen, and Linda.

Our Human Angels

During their 11-year evolution, Tom and Carol have had some human "angels" enter their life as well. These are very close friends who have helped with so many things and it shows how much they really do care. A very special thanks to April, Louis, and Ahrynn.

Interpreting the Photographs

The authors have selected these photographs from thousands they have taken principally in 2011 and 2012. Except for a few, the majority of these photos were taken in Northern California. In some sections there will be a story to accompany the photograph to tell perhaps what it means to the authors or how it came to be taken. Other photographs will have a suggestion of a meditation phrase. In this way, the book's photographs can serve as a meditation tool for daily meditations. Many images in these photographs seem to have a face or faces that appear to be humanlike, or even look like an animal, or even an alien-type creature. When you look at the cloud images, look for faces, eyes, noses, mouths and also bodies, legs, arms, feet, fingers. This will help you to digest the image that is being sent. It is also suggested you look through the book more than once because you will likely see more or you may see better, either close up or by holding the photographs at a distance. The authors believe there is some intelligence guiding these images in the clouds. Surely, all these images in these photographs could not be mere coincidence. So this raises questions: How is this done? Who is doing it? Why are they being presented in this manner? What is being communicated to us? What is the message?

Presentation of Photographs

The presentation of the photos in this book is prepared so the reader can best see the images that have been found by the authors. There has been no manipulation or fabrication of any of the images in these photographs. Many of the photographs have been enhanced only through color contrast so the images can be better seen. Nearly all of the photographs were taken by a Nikon 300 camera, however, some were taken by an Apple iPhone.

Foreward

No one can ever forget the wonder of childhood when we lay on our backs and watched the summer clouds floating overhead. We would call out to friends what we saw in the sky and compare notes as to what each saw in a particular cloud. A common thing we tended to see was "God on his throne," or cherubs. The sky was our nearest thing to actually seeing God in our youthful minds. But, as adults, we can recapture the wonder, excitement and nearness to Spirit as we once again lift our eyes on our walks and nature tours and experience all the splendor and wonder of clouds.

There will always be the skeptics who say that we project onto clouds what we want to see, much like the ink blot tests of psychologists. Maybe we do, or maybe Spirit just gives creation a nudge once in a while so we remember things beyond our daily lives. In this book, many of the clouds have taken on the forms of angels. It is hard to find individuals who do not believe in angels and these wonderful cloud pictures taken by Tom and Carol bring to mind the winged creatures of the Heavens. What could present a more soaring and inspirational picture than a cloud that brings to mind an angel looking over and down on us.

At times of sorrow and depression, anxiety and fear, nature is often the greatest healer. As we call out to Spirit in these times, "Mother Earth" and "Father Sky" often provide clues to our recovery. If we look up and see angelic forms in the clouds, we can believe there is something greater in our lives and that we are loved and cared for by invisible guardians. We don't have to be children to believe this.

Most of us imagine angels through the archetypal perspective of white luminous beings with wings, halos, flowing dresses and harps of gold. However, the earliest creatures with wings of which we are aware came from Mesopotamian sculptures that later influenced Egyptian art and then Christian perceptions of guardian beings.

Angels can appear to us in the usual stereotyped form or in other ways. Each person recognizes angels differently. Tom saw with his vision of St. Michael through the archetype of how Christian artists perceived St. Michael with his sword. We may just see forms of light. Some people are not visionary and experience angelic forces through the hearing of a voice, thoughts or feelings.

In my own thirty years of spiritual pursuit, healing work and clairvoyant experiences, I have experienced angelic forces in many ways. I think that angels can act through human beings or can appear in all kinds of forms. Angelic forces can radiate through animals. Deceased members of our family or ancestors can be our guardians. I remember one experience in a snow storm when my car got stuck in a deserted warehouse district at night. I could not get my car up the hill, which was icy. I kept trying to drive up the slope and slid right back down. This was before cell phones and I rapidly reached near hysteria. Suddenly I felt a gentle spirit slap across my face (like one would do to a hysterical person) and the words came to me telepathically to slowly try to drive up the hill again. This time I made it up the slope and safely reached home. This is an episode of angelic intervention that I will never forget.

Tom's spiritual experience of hearing the voice of Archangel Michael when he was in a car accident and later seeing him in the clouds set him on a journey that he never expected to take. Spirit chose a creative way to lead Tom into greater depths of spirituality and the ability to see God's messages in the clouds and through his remarkable art. We can all be grateful for Tom, his creative abilities, his skills in photography and most of all his love and willingness to share.

I have never met Tom in person, but we have a lively and ongoing email correspondence about everything spiritual. A mutual friend gave us each other's email addresses a few years ago at a time when we were both marketing our new books. I feel like I know Tom very well as he has shared his thoughts, visions, art work and cloud books with me. His generosity in giving to others shows his charitable inclinations and desire to share. He is a teacher of spirituality with his art and images as he helps our spirits to soar.

When you view Tom's third book, which is smaller and can easily be slipped into a handbag, take time with each picture. What does the cloud form say to you? What does it touch inside? Does it stimulate you to take a rest and meditate? Do you feel the joy course through your inner being? This is a wonderful book for both contemplation and meditation –and especially prayer. Treasure each picture as a chance to take an inward journey and to be grateful for our magnificent skies. Say thanks to Tom each time you experience Creation and the Angels through his eyes!

My own transformation happened in 1980 when I was a member of the Church of Jesus Christ of Latter-day Saints. I had a spontaneous kundalini experience and the energy zoomed up my spine and left me clairvoyant, clairaudient, clairsentient, and with healing abilities. I had no reference point from which to understand what had happened to me with my Mormon acculturation. I also had a vision, much like Tom, at this time. A being of great light appeared to me and said he was a "savior" from another planet. Of course I could not comprehend that at the time and decided it must have been Jesus. But this being has been a guardian and guide to me for 32 years. He is my "angel." Other people have also had appearances of luminous beings who claim to be extra-terrestrial and there to help, teach and protect. So, again, angels come in many forms. My own story of transformation, angels, and ascension is told in the book below.

Reverend Judith M. McLean, Ph.D.
Sanctuary11@comcast.net

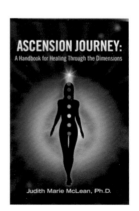

Author of *Ascension Journey: A Handbook for Healing Through the Dimensions*

This book can be purchased on Amazon.com at the link below; through Kindle, Apple products and from the publisher, CreateSpace.com.

http://www.ascensionjourney.com

Why This Book and What is Angelic?

Through the years, Tom and Carol have assembled so many cloud photographic images that appear angelic or guide you to believe that the image was created by angelic beings. This book perhaps raises your consciousness about what is truly angelic or what are angels. They are hoping this book could give you some insight and information that will perhaps help make your own decisions about angels and creation, perhaps bring you closer to angels, or perhaps for you to find your own angel.

So what is angelic? So many things come to mind and through history much has been written. Probably most of us identify angels as having big wings, floating or flying in the air, or perhaps with robes or a very bright light. Also, angels may be considered to be very powerful, may be considered to be messengers or servants of God. Many people think of angels as very loving, incredibly beautiful, have healing abilities, and very peaceful creatures. Creatures that bring miracles to humans – creatures that have brought guidance over the centuries. Beings that are honest, have integrity, have no jealousy, no greed, no envy, no selfishness and perhaps no ego. As the reader, perhaps you will begin to think of terms that might describe angels from your perspective.

 One of the reasons why this chapter is being written is for you to consider how you can be angelic, because humans can be angels in their own way. You can be of service to others in need. You can be an inspiration to a little boy or little girl or to anyone you encounter. You could be a leader for others to follow in an angelic way. You can take responsibility as an angel might. You can fill yourself with love, not hate. You can purge all negatives from your mind and your heart. You can consider love for all of creation.

What We Believe

Tom and Carol believe that there are many dimensions of existence. Earth is what might be called the third dimension – a dimension where the reality is formed by solid objects, like our bodies or the earth. Many believe that there is at least one universe and maybe many more. Quantum scientists are now considering that there are multi-universes. Perhaps they are right. Tom and Carol believe that there is a Creator. Many call it the Source, many call it God, and many religions have other names for the entity that created all that exists. Tom and Carol believe we must honor it. Tom and Carol believe in angels that are a part of the other dimensions. They also believe in angels as messengers, as loving beings, that give us guidance for us to follow the right path. They believe in good and evil – perhaps dark and light. They believe each of us have a choice whether to follow a good or evil path. And most of all, Tom and Carol believe that LOVE is the meaning of life, all that matters, and why each of us is here on Earth.

Ways to be Angelic!

Simple Messages from Tom and Carol

This book is about angelic images and messages in the sky. These perhaps bring into focus what is truly angelic. Here, in the following five sections, Tom and Carol suggest ways to be a little more angelic in your life.

Simply "Thank You"

It is important to talk about the issue of simply being thankful or being in gratitude for all that each of us have. With the more recent progression of our culture and society and with the addition of so much technology [websites, emails, texting, facebooks, smartphones], it is our experience that many people are not as "connected" as they may think – especially as compared to the time prior to so much technology. How many times each day have you seen people sitting together as if they were meeting, yet they were so absorbed with their phones, emails and texting? It now seems to be a common practice – where people are seen together eating at a restaurant or cafe, yet they are eating and reviewing their emails and texts at the same time, while ignoring the other person. While this technology has its benefits, it feels like we are losing some of the human closeness we used to have and an appreciation of each other. How are we paying attention to the other people in our lives that we are with at any moment when we are texting or phoning?

Additionally, with technology, we seem to be losing the art of handwriting. People now communicate on devices like computers and mobile phones where the "typed" word is the format. For example, what if the United States Constitution was done on computer or via email and that was the only source of it? What feeling would you get from looking at it typed vs looking at it in its original handwriting? When something is written in someone's handwriting, it is more personal and special. When it is typed, it lacks a personal touch, and in fact, it could be from someone other than the real author.

Another example is seen when finding old letters between friends or loving partners. To see and read such letters in their own handwriting is more personal and means so much more than to see typed letters. In the future, will love letters only be typed or texted?

Another similar aspect of this decline in human closeness and handwriting is that we are losing the art of "thank you." We find in our experience that a simple thank you has disappeared. Thank you by voice over the phone and more importantly in the written fashion has declined to a point of a rarity. For example, it has become all too rare to receive a written thank you note in the mail.

So it is our hope that you will read this and perhaps consider thanking people, thanking your family members, thanking your friends, and even a stranger that may be helping you. Thank them face-to-face, and with handwritten notes showing your love for them. Love is the one thing that binds us all together.

Thank You

Lead with Your Heart

It is our belief that the HEART and LOVE are so important to us as human beings and our souls. The hearts are in this book because they are the essence of being angelic. You will see two hearts in the next few pages – first a heart that came after the Star Gate cloud was formed in France. The Heart appeared by two sandworms coming together perfectly to form a heart at the St. Malo Beach. When we first saw it, it was incredible and we had to take a picture, and it is here for you to enjoy. The other heart is a glowing red stone carved in a heart shape that we found on a nearby road on the asphalt. What was so important is that it was so brightly glowing like it was entirely lit from within. We couldn't help but stop and take that picture and take that heart home with us. Both of these Hearts are so representative of the angelic within us as human beings that we wanted to share them.

As our adventure has evolved since 2001, one of the most important lessons we have learned is how important the HEART and LOVE is for us as a species on this planet. You probably already know, but we want to remind you that for each of us, as we are growing within our moms, that the first organ to be formed is the heart. We are heart-centered creatures – not brain-centered. As such, the heart becomes the most important part of us. Much has been written through history about the heart and what it means. Think about it. We take our heart for granted, unless it causes us problems generally as we get older. The heart is more than just an organ pumping blood, which is certainly important. But the heart is everything within us – it is our soul, it is our meaning and what we are on this planet. It is about the love we have within us. It is the meaning of life. Especially, if we can embrace such things as Divine Love – the Love of all things created whether ugly or beautiful, big or small, black or white, whatever – it doesn't matter – LOVE FOR EVERYTHING THAT HAS BEEN CREATED.

We want to convey the importance of – the Heart. Some of us really act and make decisions with our heart. Many of us probably do not – and thus make decisions entirely from the brain. This is a huge distinction.

Here are some examples. If you acted from the Heart, you might act differently during an argument, since your Heart would make sure that you don't say something so terrible you might regret later. You know, those words that are stored in your brain and you never should use against anyone. But in the heat of the moment they come out. And when they are out, the person you are talking to will never be able to forgive those words or forget them being used. By using the Heart, the Heart would prevent the brain from using them. In many ways, the Heart is so much smarter than the brain.

Or if you owned a business, and you had to lay off some employees, would you lay them off just before Christmas, or wait until a better time. The Heart would wait, of course.

Or if you had so much money that you could not use it all nor could your family – would you use that money just to keep for yourself and family, or use some of it to help others that are more needy? The Heart says to be in service to those in need.

If you encountered a "homeless person" laying on the sidewalk, would you walk by in disgust or just turn your head away? Or give that person some money to help him or her at that moment? The Heart would direct you to help in some way.

Or when you are doing something you knew would physically or emotionally hurt someone, would you go through with it or decide to stop it before it could do the damage? Of course, your Heart would make you stop.

Or when winning is all there is! We are all taught to win, and that winning is all so important and all that matters. It could be in an athletic game, in an argument or similar circumstance. But perhaps winning is not everything. Your Heart may want to "allow" someone else to win for a change. Perhaps to make the other person happy, to show your love, or boost his or her ego a bit, or simply to just be nice. Tom will never forget the lesson taught to him at 11 years old by his Little League coach Eddie. It was the last game of the season and Tom's team, the Indians, was 11 – 0 and it was very likely that the team would win the last game to be 12 – 0. But at the start of the game, Eddie decided to put in the worst players so that the Indians would lose. Eddie was brilliant and always used his Heart. That lesson of losing was to show caring for the other team's players, and to show the Indian team players that winning is not everything. Tom still remembers that day 50 years later and has used that lesson throughout his life.

The list is endless with situations such as those above. Each day we are faced with decisions that challenge our brain and our Heart. Think about it.

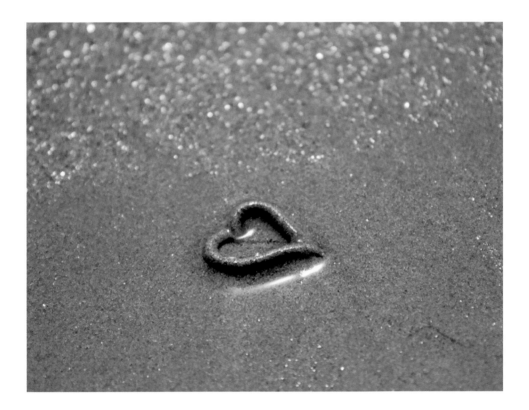

Make Peace Within Yourself

Many of us pray to the angels for Peace on Earth. But it seems our human history is filled with conflict between people – within families, communities, between nations, and certainly between races, and religions. To us, Peace is the essence of being in the state of the Angelic.

Why is it so hard to have peace? Perhaps these conflicts arise over jealousy, as in the story of Cain and Abel or perhaps over greed within families when the "Will" is read. Perhaps it is over the profit motive in businesses and corporations. There are so many instances of it. Why is peace so elusive? Peace perhaps scares people. Actually, none of us have ever lived in a world of peace. We really don't know what it is. We certainly don't know what it feels like. Many of us have not seen peace in our own families. If you read local papers or the internet news every day, there is no peace. Instead we are brought the everyday list of killings, torture, drugs, rapes, sexual abuse, and conflicts on a global basis. This is not Peace but often we feel helpless to change it.

We believe that the only way to effect a change towards worldwide Peace is on a personal basis. If we do not have "inner peace" or peace within ourselves, how can we expect to have worldwide peace?

Peace

The key to inner peace from our perspective is to use the Heart to change yourself within. With the Heart actuated so to speak, perhaps each of us could find a way to love ourselves first. With the Heart, perhaps each of us could remove the greed, jealousy, hatred, intolerance, and the large ego that may be within us. If so, these traits could be removed and replaced with pure love for ourselves and for others, and for our whole planet. Imagine a state of Love within each of us! A state of mind that would love instead of hate, that would be tolerant of all situations and people, that would not place money above all other things, that giving was so much better than taking, and to believe that our egos could be tempered to allow others into our lives.

There is no quick solution for Peace. But imagine if you as one person could attain a state of Peace [and the Love that goes with it] within you, wouldn't that be enough? Imagine living each day in appreciation for all that you are and all that you have. Imagine helping others less fortunate all the time because it is easy and fulfilling. Imagine the thankfulness you might have for just living on planet Earth, appreciating your sense of sight to see the colorful landscape or to peer into another's eyes, to wonder about the blue skies and white clouds, appreciating your sense of smell to breathe the scent of the air, your sense of touch to feel physical objects or even another person's skin, to let all your senses appreciate that river, sea, or ocean, to be able to "think", analyze, and imagine things with your incredible brain. But what is so incredible is that, you, as one person, has the ability to Love and Care and to share it with as many people, animals, insects, and plants as you wish. That is real Power! More power than any leader or corporate president because there is nothing anyone can do to stop or control you in your exercise of Love.

So you can have Peace on Earth! It is your personal peace with yourself and all that you may choose to do in your lifetime. It is your expression of LOVE that allows you to have inner peace. These are the decisions that only you can make. All of us have these distinct choices in our lives. There is no one else to blame if each of us does not choose inner peace and love.

A Dose of Kindness

Another aspect of being in a state of the angelic is how you might interact with other people, animals, the plant world and other inhabitants of this planet.

We think that most of us have experienced a very kind person in our lives. Due to that person's kindness, we remember that person forever. It could have been a teacher, parent, friend, or just someone we met for the first time.

So kindness is so important in our lives. Kindness goes a long way even if shown by only one person to another. One act of kindness can stimulate others to be kind as well. We should always strive to be kind. The rewards are a sense of love and inner peace that cannot be achieved in any other way than to live in a state of kindness. It is often better to be kind than to be right.

Kindness can be found in a smile, nice loving words, a loving gesture, the tone of the voice, and our language.

One of the lessons we have learned is to not live an everyday life of negativity. We try to not invite any sort of negativity into our lives and if it enters our lives, we remove it quickly. Negativity could be in the form of people, TV, radio, driving on the freeway, or at a party. The list is endless. It is a constant struggle to reduce, control, and eliminate negativity around you because it is so pervasive in our world. But everyday, we make it a point to focus on being positive. It feels so much better when we live this way. We cannot live any other way now.

We found a quote in the book *The Monks and Me* by Mary Paterson. The quote is just perfect. "Let no one ever come to you without leaving better and happier. Be the expression of God's kindness: kindness in your face, kindness in your eyes, kindness in your smile."

Tolerance

Another important aspect of the angelic is Tolerance. It seems in our fast paced world that we have less and less tolerance for so many things. Being in such a state of quick actions, responses, and immediate satisfaction to so many stimuli is exactly the opposite of living in the angelic.

Tolerance, in an angelic way, might be to slow down, be very patient with all things you do, to pray, and to meditate. The most important action you can take is to take time out for you. Additionally, take time for you with your family or partner or friends. Enjoy life, read a book, take a jog, and have fun. There are so many things you can do to slow down. Most of us struggle with slowing down against the pace of our society. But it is very important for our well-being, the health of our mind and body.

Tolerance, in an angelic way, also means allowing our prejudices to recede or be eliminated from our lives. This may be tough as we are taught so many things growing up and we all have all kinds of experiences in our culture. However, tolerance of others is so important to living in a state of grace, kindness, caring, and loving.

Tolerance means accepting of others who may be a different race, different color, speak a different language, who practice a different religion, who may be too skinny or too fat, who look different, who might have more money or material wealth, who have different ideas, and who are too tall or too short. The point is that differences should not matter and that there should be acceptance in our society.

Now we all encounter "bad" things that another person might do to you. They might bully you, or want to just beat you up. They might want to spread lies about you. They might want to take your job or see you fired. Some people are just mean-spirited. Others wallow in cliques in the pursuit of telling stories everyday about others that are supposedly not up to their values or stature. Such behavior is just human nature and you can participate in it or you can take care of your own life.

It is a waste of time and energy to live a life worrying about or hating people that are different than you. It just does not matter if you are living your life as you wish. If you are busy living your own life, you should have no time to think about or even act upon negative beliefs. It may be a bit crass, but the old saying "Mind Your Own Business" is a good rule of thumb. If you are tending to the business of your own life and your family, you will have quite enough to do.

It may be tough to do, but each of us can look deep inside of themselves and analyze who they are, what they do, and what they believe. If one finds that he or she has some negative traits, perhaps this is an opportunity he or she can try to change their beliefs and their behavior. No one is perfect and we all have room to improve.

Open your heart and you will see

Hope

There is a song that was sung by Frank Sinatra called "High Hopes" which expresses the point of having hope despite the worst of obstacles. Being angelic means understanding and using your power as one person to overcome any obstacle. It means not to have despair when it would be so easy. It means doing something positive that you want to do when all others around you are saying you cannot do it.

Embracing hope is so important to our well-being and to spreading hope to those around us. If you can bring hope to the world, then peace and love will follow.

Choices

A Poem by Tom Lumbrazo

We can grow or we can stagnate

We can build or we can destroy

We can let fear rule us or be fearless

We can bully or we can help others

We can be greedy or we can give

We can judge others or we can accept all

We can take advantage or we can help

We can have prejudice or we can be tolerant

We can kill or we can defend

We can lie or we can take responsibility

We can follow or we can lead

We can hold grudges or we can forgive

We can hate or we can love...

Divine Love is the answer!

Tom and Carol's Real Cloud Stories

This chapter contains twelve true stories in which cloud messages have come to Tom and Carol to experience and to share with you. Once you have read them, you will likely wonder how such amazing impossible events could happen, why they happened, and who could have made these clouds.

Archangel Michael

The beginning of an unexpected spiritual path began on February 9, 2001, when Tom was driving down Highway 65 in Placer County at 60mph on a four-lane expressway. Out of nowhere came a very strong male voice that said "Slow to 35." It was so strong, and it was coming from the front passenger seat area. As Tom heard this message, he certainly wondered what was that, but his intuition said follow it, so he slowed to 35.

Almost immediately, a car with three young men passed by very fast and went up to the next stop light that was hundreds of feet ahead. The light was showing green and yet their car stopped at the green light. As Tom approached he wondered what they were doing, and as he approached closer, they pulled right in front of him making a perpendicular move to the left and stopping in front of his Jeep. He had no option but to hit them. Both cars were demolished and both cars were pushed through the intersection. While everyone had injuries, they were not life threatening.

When the CHP arrived ten minutes later, Tom told the story to the policeman and he said "Mister, if you were going 60, you would be dead right now."

That led Tom to thinking this was very special – Why was I saved? Who saved me? What was this all about? This whole incident started a process over the last 11 years to search for what happened and why it happened.

About four years later, Tom started having visions while awake [not dreams] in the middle of the night. The very first vision was of an angel. That angel showed Tom his appearance in complete color and HD quality. The first glimpse was him in profile with huge wings, and then he turned his head to look at Tom. He was so beautiful. The second image was of the same angel on his horse with full armament and his sword.

The next day, Tom was drawn to go to the bookstore and see about angels. The very first book that he chose was of angels, and he randomly turned to the middle and there was the same image in an illustration of the angel on his horse with a sword. It was Archangel Michael. Tom started to have clues about what and who this was who saved him in 2001. In May 2008, Carol and Tom were in Sedona, Arizona, walking a large labyrinth at the St. Andrews Episcopal Church at around noon. Tom looked up and the clouds were growing and a few minutes later he had to stop and get his camera because the angel had arrived in the cloud formation. Tom and Carol were in awe of what they were seeing.

Archangel Michael was in the sky on his horse now in a cloud form, and this is the picture of that day in Sedona for you to enjoy. Tom got his documentation in a cloud photo of the angel that saved his life.

Tom felt at that moment that no one could deny what had happened to him over the last seven years because he had photographic evidence of the angel.

Star Gate

Before Carol and Tom went to England and France in the spring of 2008, one of Tom's psychic friends told him to look for a Star Gate that would be presented to him in France. The friend said that it would be guarded by two angels and to honor it, but she could not identify how it would be presented or what it would look like.

As they arrived at a place called St. Malo in France, clouds were forming overhead. Tom first saw some little clouds that looked like tiny angels, and then there was a big head with a big eye. Tom started to wonder what was happening.

Next Tom saw what looked like a being with his hands out like he was flying à la Superman and over to the right is a little character in the clouds that has his head and chin resting on his hands, like taking it all in.

Above all of these clouds, Tom saw this incredible creature that had a head, a body, two legs, arms, and most importantly it had one arm with his hand and finger pointing downward. It is so clear. It reminded Tom of the Predator character in the movie Predator. It was pointing down for a reason because downward was the STAR GATE – a precise cloud in a triangle form. Imagine a cloud with a triangular hole cut out so you could see through it. There appears to be an angel above the Star Gate cloud. It was so immense and it was over the commercial downtown area of St. Malo. While Tom was standing on the public sidewalk taking lots of pictures, he felt as if time had stopped. It was so special, and so surreal. Many people were walking by as Tom was taking pictures of this huge STAR GATE cloud, but none looked up at where Tom was pointing his camera. That was so very unusual, as the cloud was so huge in the sky. Nonetheless, the STAR GATE appeared and the angels appeared. Could it be that the STAR GATE was a vortex to another dimension?

Santa Claus Comes to Town

Carol and Tom went to a children's fundraiser about ten miles from their house in the beginning of July 2011. As they came to the event and parked the car, they both got out and Carol noticed a strange cloud in the north sky. It was small and fuzzy. So, Tom got his camera and pointed it at this cloud and zoomed in with his lens. He couldn't believe his eyes. It was Santa Claus with a sleigh and a couple of reindeer. He could tell instantly it was Santa because his hat was so distinctly that of images of Santa Claus. It was so amazing to see this in the sky – Santa Claus, supposedly a fictional character, was here with us in a cloud form. Tom took as many pictures as he could before the cloud evaporated. As you can imagine, Tom and Carol couldn't stop talking about this cloud the rest of the day.

Later that year, Tom had the idea to make the Santa photographs into a Christmas card. He enlarged the images and made a Christmas card with the words on the front "Do you believe in Santa Claus?" and on the back are photos of Carol and Tom at three years old and they say, "We do." They ordered 1,000 copies and also emailed it all around. They emailed the Christmas card and its story to many of the large media outlets, television stations locally and nationally, as well as large newspaper outlets in the country, with no response. All of them probably thought Tom and Carol were crazy or that they PhotoShopped the images. Tom and Carol emailed the card to all of their friends. Also, they would take copies of it and walk down the sidewalk in their town or go into a store and go up to people and say, "Do you believe in Santa Claus?" Amazingly, 99% of these people said, "Yes." Then Tom and Carol would give them the Santa card. All the people that saw it were so excited and so happy to see confirmation that there truly might be a Santa Claus for all of us.

To Tom and Carol, Santa Claus is a form of an angel who brings joy and happiness to so many around the world each year.

Do you belive in Santa Claus?

Tom Cumbrazo ©
whenangelstouch.com

We Still Do!

Merry Christmas and Happy New Year
from Tom and Carol Lumbrazo

Actual Photo taken in Lincoln, CA July 2011
© www.WhenAngelsTouch.com

Tom Cumbrazo
whenangelstouch.com

Hands of God

In June 2011, Tom woke up on a beautiful summer morning and went outdoors with his coffee to read the paper. As he sat on his large deck outdoors, he noticed how clear and blue the sky was – not a cloud anywhere to be seen. And as Tom was reading the paper, all of a sudden, there was a voice in his head and it said clearly – so simply – "LOOK UP NOW."

Tom has gotten used to this kind of thing so he wondered where to look. He did look immediately over his left shoulder. To his surprise, Tom saw these two clouds, side by side, that were the image of giant hands and arms. Tom was so amazed, he ran into the house to get his camera and took many pictures.

The hands were so precisely done and formed. What did it mean? There could be many meanings, but to Tom it is a comfort to know that these gigantic hands are there to comfort him and others. Maybe to show us that there is a loving presence on this planet.

Journey to the Navajo Indian Lands

In 2011, Carol and Tom took care of his parents as they were quite ill and eventually they passed in the summer of 2011. Earlier in 2011, Tom had gone to a doctor's office with his Mom and noticed this magazine in the lobby that showed the new hotel in the Monument Valley Navajo Lands located in northern Arizona. It looked so amazing. You may know this area of the Navajo lands. It was the setting of many movies with its beautiful desert scenery. Tom thought maybe one day he would be able to go there.

After his Mom passed in September 2011, Tom and Carol decided to go to the San Francisco Giants baseball game at the end of the month. Tom also asked Carol if perhaps they should soon go to the Navajo lands and enjoy the hotel. Carol felt really concerned that winter was coming and they might get snowed in. She asked Tom to consider postponing it to 2012 and Tom agreed. At the day of the Giants game, Tom and Carol met their good friend Alan in San Francisco. As they were having lunch together, Tom told Alan the story of going to Monument Valley and postponing it to 2012. Since Alan is very "intuitive," it was not a surprise that he started to "channel." He said, "THE ELDERS ARE SAYING YOU MUST GO TO THE NAVAJO NATION NOW." Knowing of Alan's abilities so well, she knew that he was probably right. She agreed to go.

Carol set up the visit for the second week of November – landing on Tom's birthday of November 11th: 11-11-2011. Tom and Carol spent several days there and had a wonderful time. Two weeks before they left, they took a long walk around their neighborhood. As they approached their house, a cloud was swirling and formed over their house. And then it manifested into this incredible Native American Indian face – perhaps that of the Navajo Indian. It was so precise with a clear blue background. It was amazing to see the cloud transform as they were viewing it.

At that moment, Tom and Carol were stunned but also had this feeling that the cloud was absolute confirmation that they must go to Monument Valley in November. Near the end of the trip in November, they got to find out the reason they were supposed to go. DIVINE LOVE!

The last night of our trip, during dinner they sat next to two women from Philadephia. The mother was 92 and her daughter was in her 60's. They were so nice to talk to during dinner, and yet Tom and Carol felt there was something mystical about them. After dinner, they said goodbye and never thought they would see them again.

Driving back to Phoenix, Tom and Carol stopped in Sedona, Arizona on November 11, 2011. That is a four-hour drive from Monument Valley. At about 5pm, they decided to have dinner at a place called Picasso's Pizza located on the outskirts of Sedona. As Tom and Carol were sitting down to eat, Tom noticed the people coming into the restaurant – the two women from Philadelphia! Tom and Carol were so surprised at this chance meeting a day later. It seemed impossible. The women did not know Tom and Carol were going to Sedona, nor when or where they were going to eat.

Tom walked up to them and they seemed so happy to see him. The mother smiled and said to Tom that she had something important to tell him. She said "You must research this...Julian of Norwich...promise me Tom that you will do this for me!" Of course, Tom agreed.

So Tom and Carol had their dinner and said goodbye to the women. Later that night, Tom did research Julian on Norwich on his iPad. Julian was a young girl of about 16, living in a church in Norwich, England around the 1300–1400s. She was dying of the plague as so many were at the time. All of a sudden, she had 16 visions of Jesus Christ. Jesus healed her and she lived into her 70s. She wrote many books on information that Jesus had passed on to her. The subject was DIVINE LOVE – a love for all things, a love for this planet, a love for all things living and not living. A love for all of creation that is here and that all of us encounter every day. This event and the research certainly made Tom and Carol think of expanding their view of love.

Tom and Carol hope that you will consider that messages come to all of us in so many ways, such as in this case. They hope that when you look at this photograph of this Native Indian face that you remember that it is all about DIVINE LOVE.

The Hawaiian God Cloud

In 2008, Carol and Tom went to Hawaii for a vacation. Before they left, Tom had visited his psychic friend. She told him that on the Big Island of Hawaii there is a place to go where the lava meets the ocean. She said that Tom and Carol should go there to see the clouds of water vapor swirl like a tornado. Tom knew that his friend has been right so many times that he must do this.

When they arrived on the Big Island, they definitely made a trip to where this lava was flowing out and hitting the ocean. It was such a beautiful sight. Tom noticed how the steam cloud was actually in a spiral like how a tornado would look and just as his friend predicted. It wasn't just steam coming up in any amorphous way, but it had a definite shape and form and it was spiraling.

As Tom and Carol watched the spiral cloud, they could see arms wanting to get out of it, even a head. So Tom kept taking pictures and all of a sudden, this incredible, big cloud formed out of it which is what Tom and Carol call the Hawaiian God. Such a precise image of a head with a hooked nose and a big belly for the body and a big arm and shoulder. Simply amazing! What would form such a steam cloud into this image?

But what was the message? Tom thinks the message was that there is life everywhere and it comes together to send us messages of comfort and love. What do you think?

The Young Girl that said "Thank You"

A friend of Tom's called him one day and asked if he could come to the hospital and help her teenage daughter, who was dying. Tom immediately went to the hospital and gave of his thoughts and energy to help the young girl. And he went again a week later. She seemed to be getting better, but after another week, she had passed. Tom was depressed that she had died. She was so young.

Two weeks later, Tom was in his back yard looking at clouds, and then this really detailed one came over his house and stayed in the same exact location for over 20 minutes. Of course, Tom took lots of photos of it.

As he looked at the photos in detail on his computer, he noticed how incredibly it matched the appearance of the young girl he met in the hospital. The cloud image had her short hair, her little nose, her face and eyes. When Tom took this photo to his psychic friend to see if she could ascertain what this was, his friend said it was definitely the girl, and that she was sending her thank you for Tom's efforts at her bedside.

Tom felt this was just another instance of love crossing the barriers of our Earth, our third dimension, this time to the afterlife.

The Message of the Tree of Life

Tom and Carol went to Egypt in 2008 and one of the things they found was the image of the Tree of Life in many of the ancient temples and buildings. The images inspired them to research the meanings of the Tree of Life. They learned that many cultures around the world had a tree of life symbol.

Then, of all things, a Tree of Life cloud image appeared one day three years later, and Tom was able to take a photo of it. It is a very strange cloud. The tree is very white yet the area around the branches is very blue. The cloud mass of the tree was very solid. It was configured with a large trunk and smaller branches as would most trees. It was quite unique.

So what does this Tree of Life Cloud mean? Why did it present itself to them? With their research of the Tree of Life in other cultures, they found some interesting meanings such as:

- Symbol of the Creator

- Manifestation of the God reality

- Represents the beginning of Mankind

- Provides warmth, protection, and food

- Bears fruit which permits immortality

Tom and Carol feel very blessed to see it and get a great photo of it to share with you.

The Eagle Cloud

One early morning Tom was awakened and as he tried to sleep, he was presented with a vision of eagles. The vision showed Tom walking up to the front porch of his house and as he looked to the left, he noticed a small hole in the ground near his house's foundation. He felt it was nothing serious and ignored it. The vision continued and showed him that next day again walking up to the porch area. He sees this hole is now about 6" wide. He quickly looks at it and feels that maybe a dog made it. As the vision continued, it showed him on the third day and again he is walking up to the porch area. He notices that hole, but now it is about 3 three feet wide. Concerned, he goes over to look at it and he cannot see a bottom to it. He now feels he has to fill it in to stop it growing. He takes a shovel and starts to fill it in from dirt from his property. It takes hours as the hole appears bottomless. Finally he filled in the hole to the top and patted it down with his shovel. Almost immediately, the dirt in the hole starts to shake. Then out comes a little baby eagle and it walks around Tom in a circle.

Then, the dirt shakes again and out comes another baby eagle. It joins the circle. And then the dirt shakes even more and out comes the much bigger mother eagle. She joins the circle with her babies. And finally, the dirt was really rumbling when out comes the huge father eagle. All the eagles then get in line and dance a circle around Tom and then walk down the walkway into the neighboring street. That's the end of the vision. Of course, Tom tells his wife Carol about this amazing and quite unique vision. He cannot get it out of his mind all morning. But in the afternoon, he was in his back yard and saw some clouds and took lots of photos. As the afternoon went on, more clouds came and almost blocked out the sun.

That evening Tom downloaded his new photos on his computer and noticed this strange one. As he looked closer, he noticed the image of an eagle from the neck, including all of its head in profile. He was amazed at the eagle's curved beak, big eye, and closed mouth. Tom wondered how his vision of the eagle that early morning had translated into a cloud with an eagle image? And what did the vision mean. What is the meaning of the eagle? According to the *Animal Spirits Guide* book by Steven D. Farmer that Tom has, it could mean a great spiritual awakening. That meaning certainly seems to fit the experiences that have happened to Tom and Carol over the last several years.

The New Baby in the Clouds

One afternoon, Tom was taking photos of the clouds on a mostly cloudy day. It seemed Tom was drawn to take them that day even though it seemed there was not much to see in the clouds.

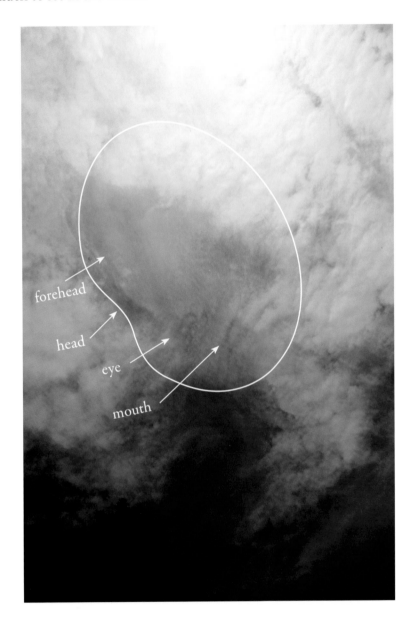

While he did not see anything in particular, when he downloaded the photos that night, he saw some incredible images of a newborn baby face in the clouds. Tom felt that this was not possible. But there it was for him to see. Tom wondered how this came to be and what the message was in the clouds that day? Perhaps, the images were sent as a reminder how precious life should be to all of us.

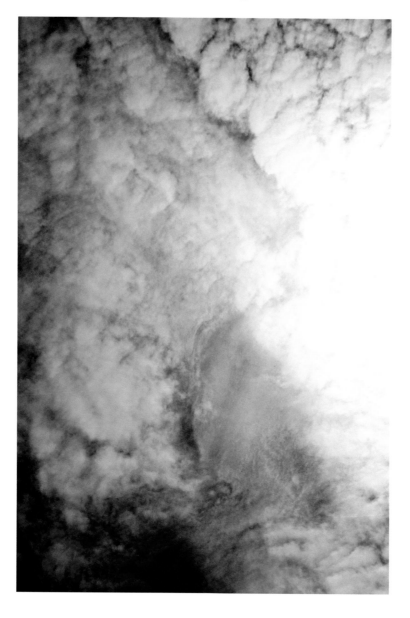

The Sword
of Archangel Michael

One spring afternoon, Tom and Carol went on a long walk in their neighborhood. As they were approaching their home about three blocks away, Tom noticed some swirling clouds up ahead and decided to take a photograph with his iPhone.

Two days later, he was looking for a photo on his iPhone and happened to see the one he recently took. He could not believe the image. The clouds he took were there, but more importantly, a wide and solid dark pink or magenta colored line came down from those clouds to the ground just in front of Tom's feet. When he analyzed the photo more closely, he was looking for a color refraction that can sometimes come in photos of the sky. But it was not that! That solid line of color went up into the clouds. In fact, Tom could see the line IN FRONT OF AND BEHIND THE CLOUDS, making it very real.

Tom later showed this photo to his psychic friend who said her guides told her it was the sword of Archangel Michael. Tom believes her interpretation, but whatever it is, it is certainly absolutely amazing!

The Divine Feminine Presence in the Sky

On a very cloudy afternoon, Tom took some cloud photos. In that time, he noticed at 12 o'clock high, some clouds of color. You know the ones that seem to have rainbow colors due to the prism effect of the sun.

Tom noticed these colored clouds and said…"What the heck…Who knows if there is something there!" So he took several photos. Later, when he downloaded his photos of the day, he came upon the colored ones. Tom was absolutely stunned at this image of a female human-like being with long legs, one long arm, chest area with breasts, and a human type head…all with some coloration. Or was this human at all? In looking at the face of this image, Tom felt it was human-looking and then again, maybe not. Nonetheless, what an incredible image in the sky, on a cloudy day!

So what does this mean! There is lots of talk in spiritual circles that the December 21, 2012 energies mean the further integration of the Divine Feminine Energies into our planet and into ourselves. Perhaps this is the answer.

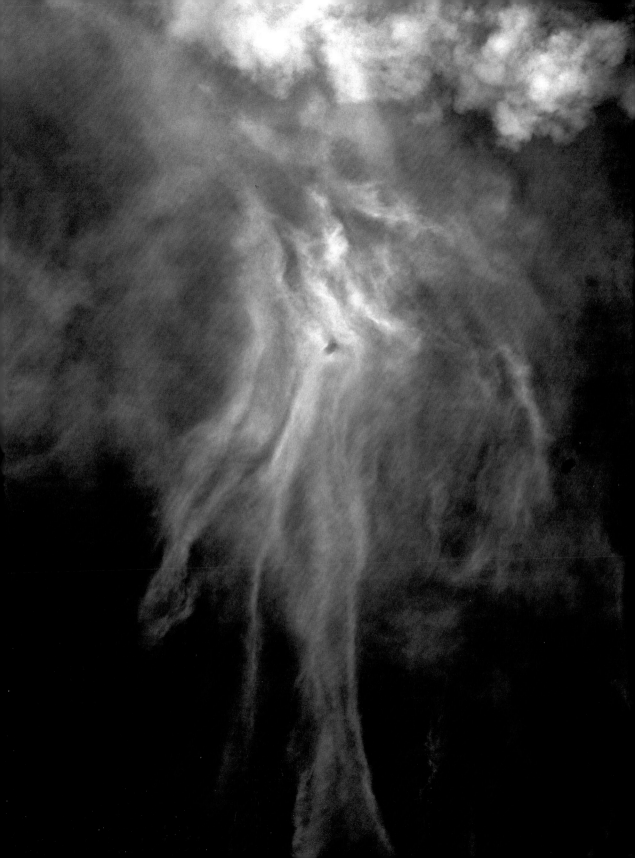

Your Stillness is the Source of all that is Beautiful

"Your Stillness is the Source of All that is Beautiful"

This statement "Your Stillness is the Source of All that is Beautiful" isn't really mine; I'm just passing on something I was given by something invisible years ago. It came to me from a voice outside of myself, in fact I remember that exact moment in 2002.

I had just moved back to Flagstaff, Arizona with my two-year-old daughter and her mother, already my ex-partner. We had left Flagstaff a year and a half earlier, to live in Paso Robles where my ex could have close loving support of her family. We didn't remain a couple from early on, which we clearly see was perfect destiny, and a pretty neat story on its own, but that's for another time. With the help of her loving family and some Angelic support we have stayed close and very connected to our child. In fact I was honored to make her wedding invitations years later.

So when we got back to Flagstaff I really wasn't seeing the beauty and magic of my life at that time. I was stuck in despair and self-judgment for what to most people would look like a messed up life; a man with no clear direction, a new child, and not being coupled with my child's mother. But some how I knew if I just kept putting one foot in front of the other, kept searching for true purpose, and kept my eyes open I would find my path.

So I'm sitting on my newly offloaded boxes in Flagstaff, positioned kind of like 'the thinker' just feeling the uncertainty and I hear a voice up to the left, not externally audible but certainly from the upper left and it said to me

"Your Stillness is the Source of All that is Beautiful!" Bam! I was blown away! So what did I do? I jumped up, I got really un-still, and wrote the phrase down and pinned it to the wall above my kitchen sink, where it sat for three years, until I brought it into my art.

The purpose I was looking for, the art, which I started in my own little gallery in downtown Flagstaff just a couple of years after getting back there. And the art I loved making and selling all began in Paso Robles, when a local vineyard invited me to create a label for them, and then rejected it for being too juvenile – it was. It gets better! That juvenile art became the art of myself and my daughter three years later when she began creating art with me at the age of five and continued to do so up until just a few years ago. And the painful life, that trip to Paso Robles, all that suffering just narrowed my focus so I could find my path in the dark, which opened my heart even more to serve with art and Love, and lead me to open a second art gallery in Nevada City, California where I met your magical author Tom and his wonderful wife Carol Lumbrazo who have been amazing examples of Love in Action for me to learn from.

Oh, "Your Stillness is the Source of All that is Beautiful" wasn't just for me, and it wasn't talking about me. It means that Still place inside of all of us, when we sit to find that Stillness and bring it our toughest questions. It will answer with a path of everything Beautiful.

Love, Light and Laughter,

Louis Buchetto

www.LouisBuchetto.com
530.368.3644

"I'm just a guy who sees sharing Love as a great way to live, so I spend much of my time refining my understanding of Love and doing what I can to be a courier of Love."

The Divine Images in the Clouds
with Words of Meditation

This section is about the many cloud images and messages that Tom and Carol have seen and captured in the sky.

Each photo will have a meditation word or phrase. In this way, you can simply view and analyze what you see in the cloud image. But also, if you wish, you can use these images as a focus of meditation. Our purpose in this book was to exhibit images that were angelic or that stimulated the mind. We hope you enjoy these cloud images and begin to realize how amazing and transformative they can be in changing or guiding your journey through life.

Divine Images
and Meditations

Meditation: Spreading Love around the world.

Meditation: Face all your obstacles and turn them into positives!

Meditation: The Power is within all of us to Love and Care.

Meditation: There is Magic in all of us to use for the Good of the Earth and all its inhabitants.

Meditation: Children know that laughter and happiness are the keys to life.

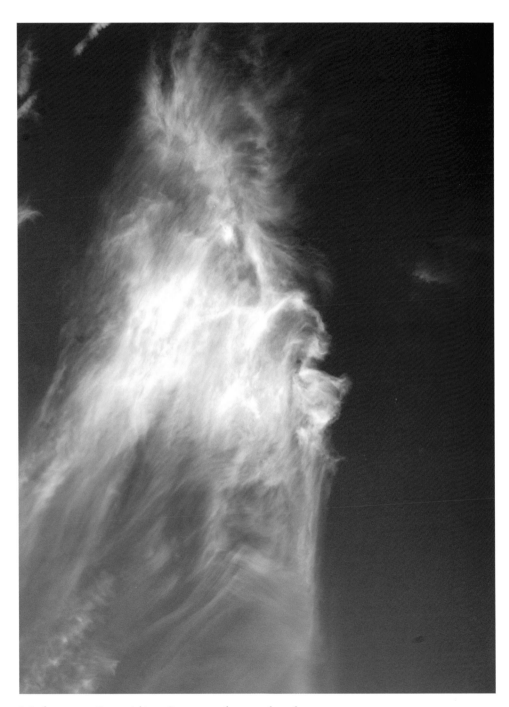

Meditation: Even Alien Creatures love to laugh.

Meditation: Look to the trees for angelic presence.

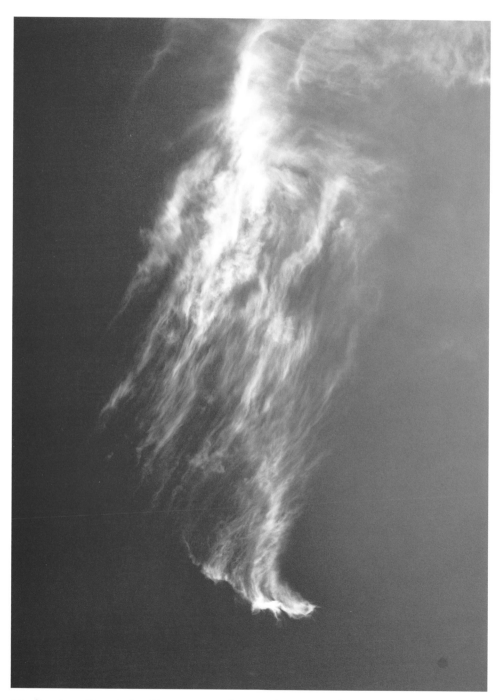

Meditation: Reach for Greatness with your Divine Soul.

Meditation: I have spread my wings to surround you in Love and Peace.

Meditation: At times, Stillness allows for connection to the Angels.

Meditation: Put on a Kind face as it is pure angelic.

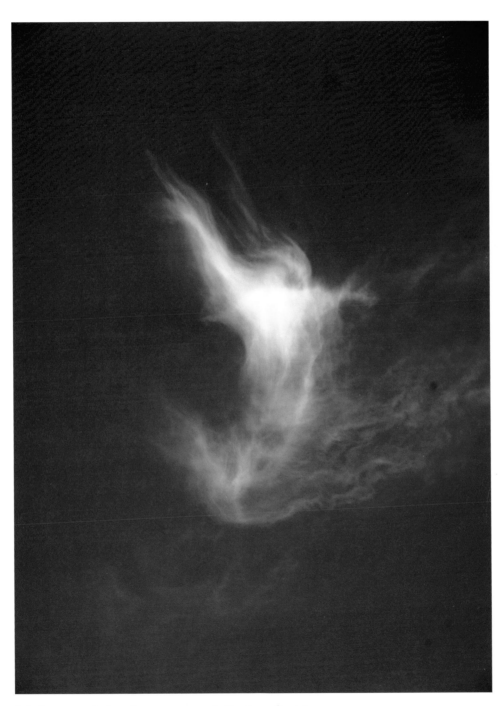

Meditation: I signal to you to seek Purity of spirit.

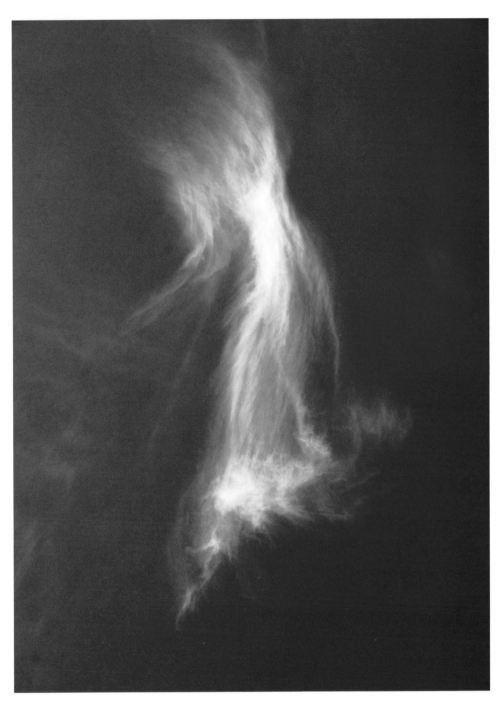

Meditation: A state of Grace is essential to a spiritual life.

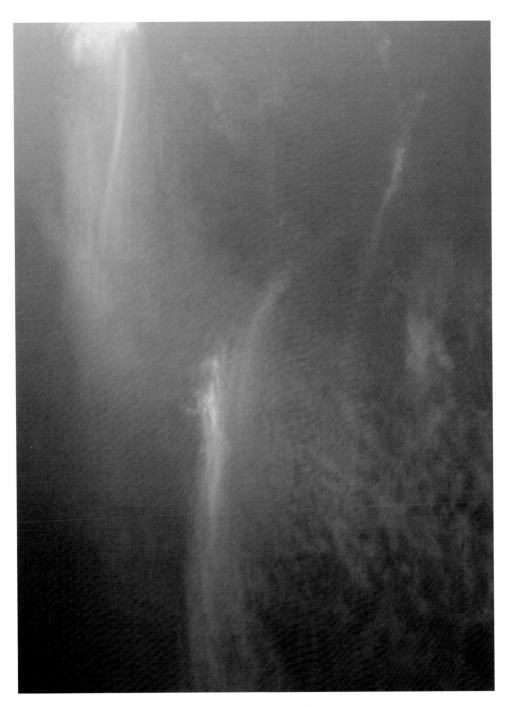

Meditation: Brilliance of your spirit shines to all you encounter.

Meditation: Embrace your Divine qualities to help others.

Meditation: It is time for all of us to lessen our Egos.

Meditation: I am so proud of you.

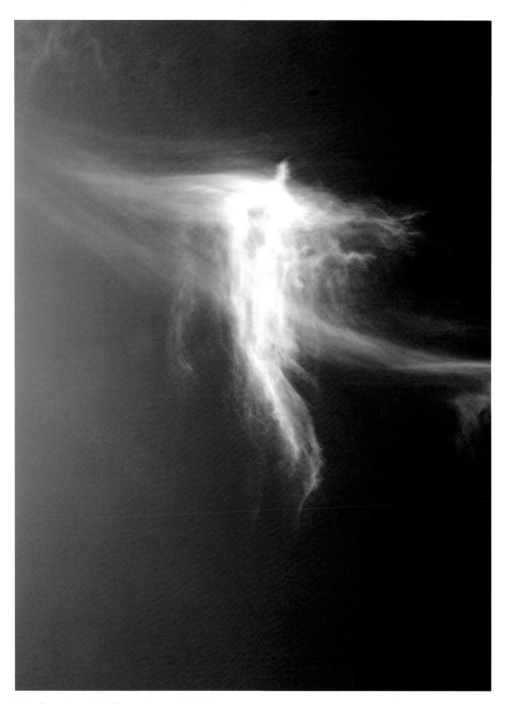

Meditation: Will you have Faith in me.

Meditation: I am amazed at your Beauty of Spirit.

Meditation: Tolerance of others that look different is working toward the angelic.

Meditation: Being small does not mean weakness.

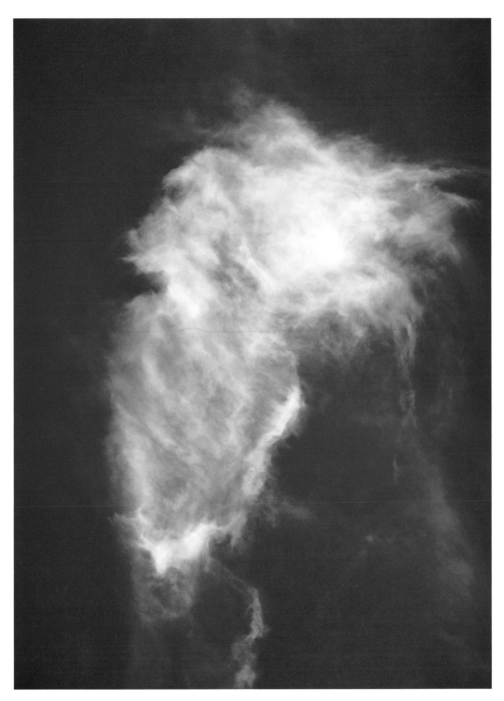

Meditation: Tranquility.

Meditation: There is Beauty in all things.

Meditation: Allow for Change in your life.

Meditation: Your angel is coming to guide you if you will only open your Heart.

Meditation: Reflection.

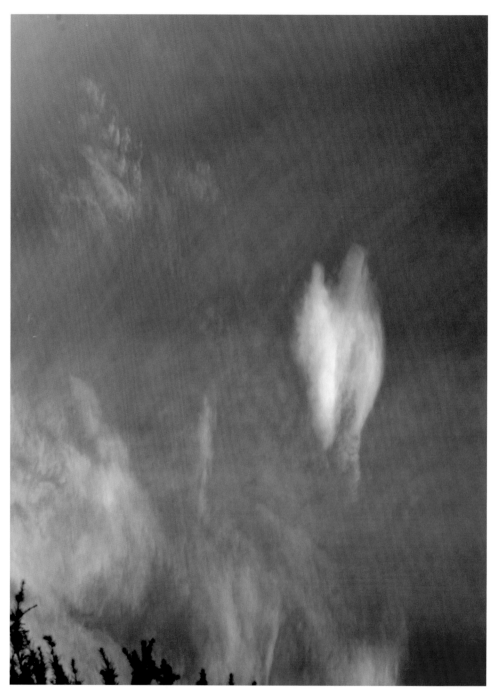

Meditation: You are never alone if you believe in angels.

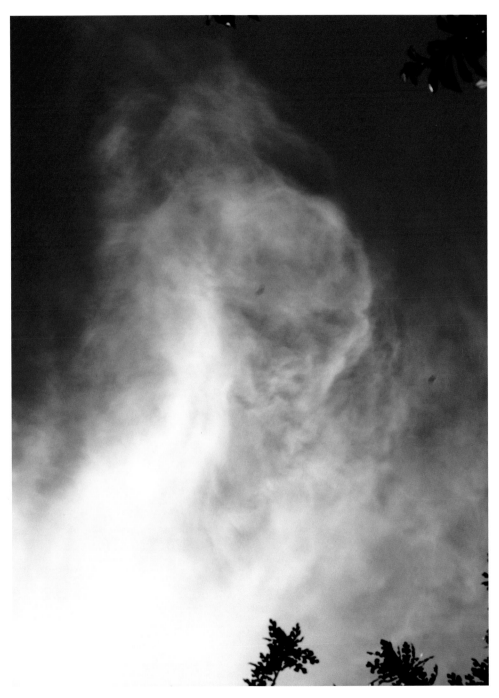

Meditation: Wisdom.

Meditation: Place your mind in a place of Grounding.

Meditation: When all of our minds are together, success will result.

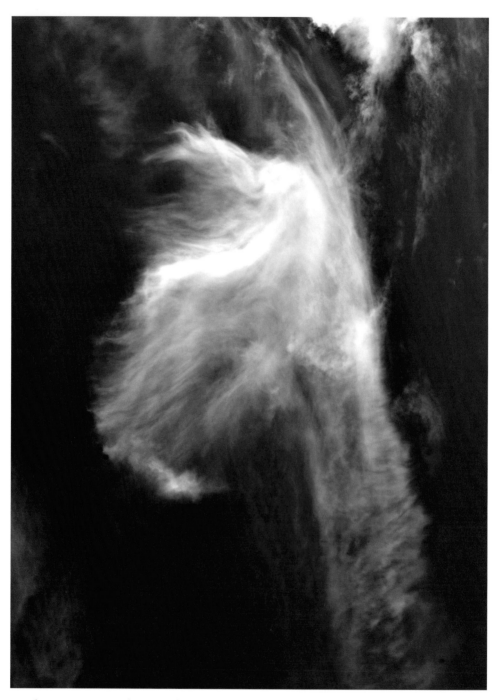

Meditation: Just Release and Relax.

Meditation: Allow yourself to just BE.

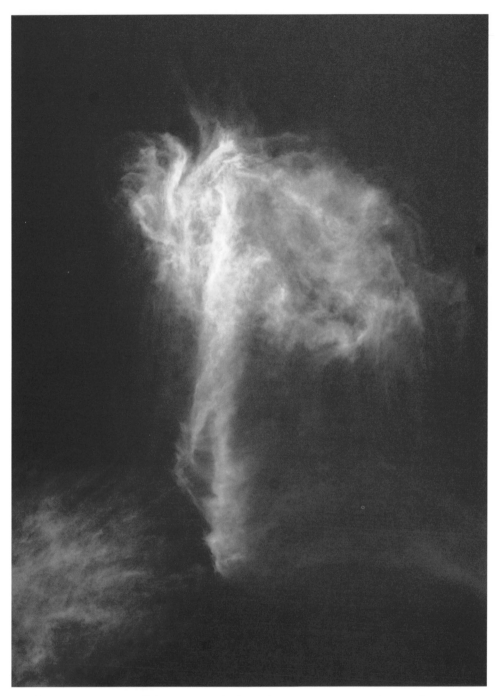

Meditation: Remove all barriers and obstacles to your spiritual growth.

Meditation: There is no place for Negativity in your life.

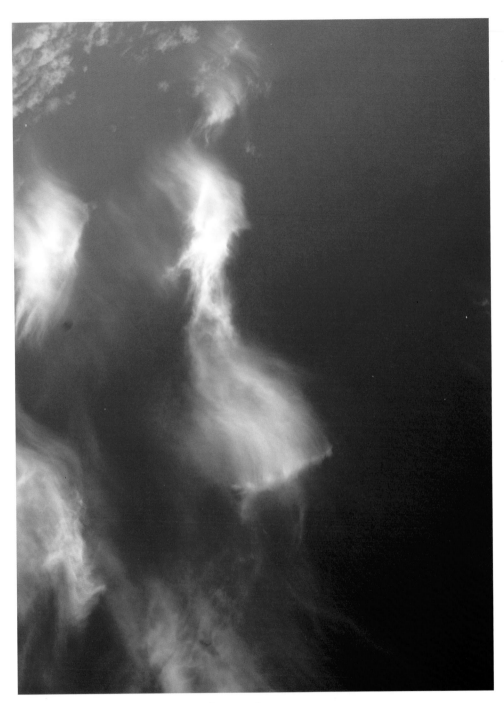

Meditation: To Love is to Love deep within you.

Meditation: Follow your guidance of the Ascended Masters.

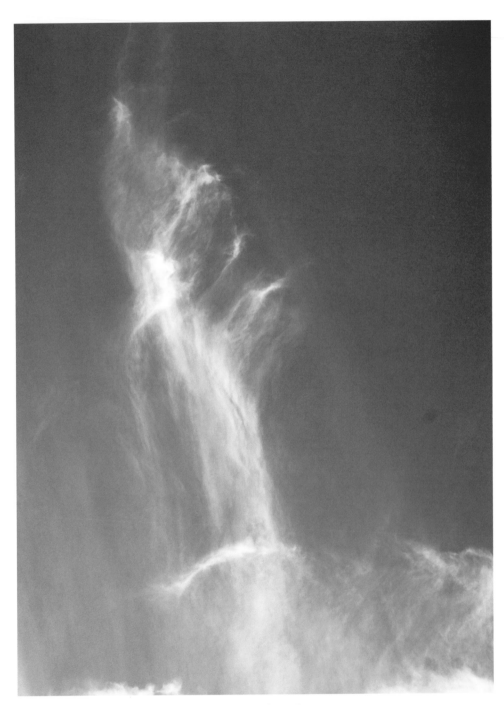

Meditation: Ascended Masters love us and guide us.

Meditation: You are the Light of your Soul.

Meditation: Harmony in your life.

Meditation: No more tears – only Happiness.

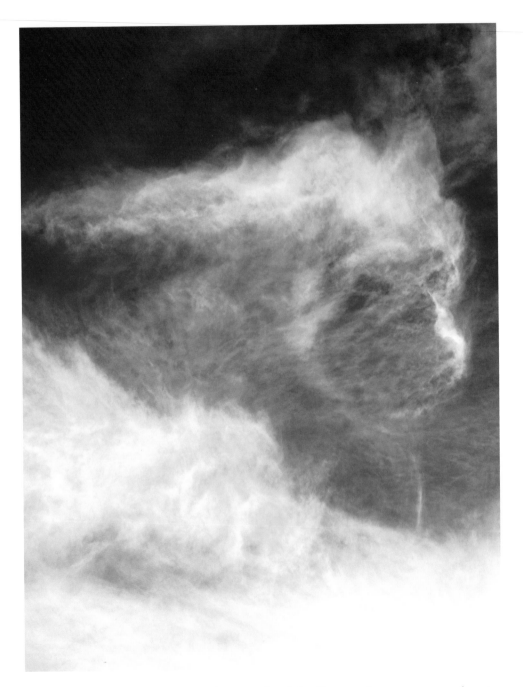

Meditation: Take the power and strength of the Bear and overcome any barrier to your success.

Meditation: Let the Angels show you the way to Divine Love and Inner Peace.

Meditation: There is the Angelic Book of the Principles of Goodness and Love and Peace – follow it.

Meditation: Stand your ground when you are working for Divine Guidance.

Meditation: There is no Fear when surrounded by Angelic Light.

Meditation: It is up to each of us to fulfill our Soul Purpose and to listen to Guidance.

Meditation: Sometimes we must shed our egos and work together for a Divine cause.

Meditation: Have the courage of the cat to do what is right rather than follow others.

Meditation: Receive the pass of angelic love and pass it on.

Meditation: All things have a Divine design and purpose and they all should be honored.

Meditation: Speak up and lead when it is the right time – have no fear.

Meditation: Have fun with anything you do in your life.

Meditation: Don't be afraid to carry your share of the responsibility.

Meditation: Believe in Dreams of Greatness, Love, and Peace.

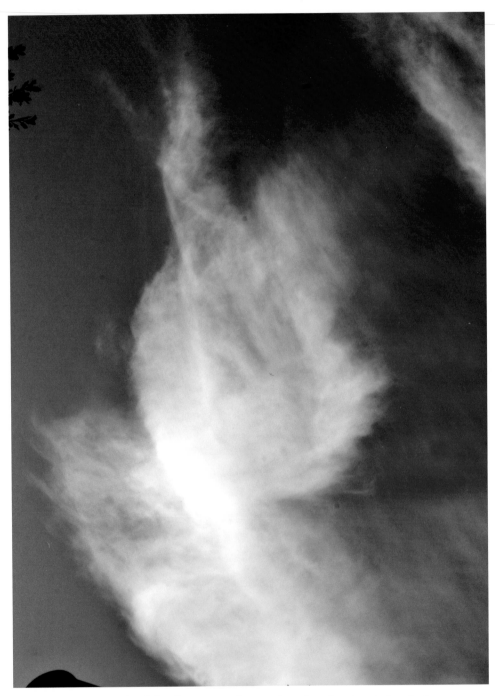

Meditation: Don't look back – move forward and make the right choices.

Meditation: Having a bad hair day – shrug it off and make certain you succeed in all that you do.

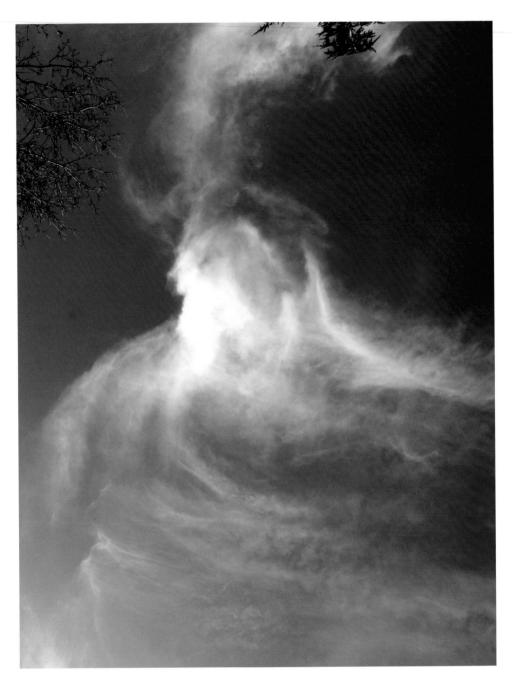

Meditation: Angels come in many forms and appearances. Accept the Divine Messages that come to you.

Meditation: You have angel wings too – only use them for good.

Meditation: Open your Heart and you will See.

Meditation: Be discerning in all that you do – someone might be in hiding trying to undo all the good you do.

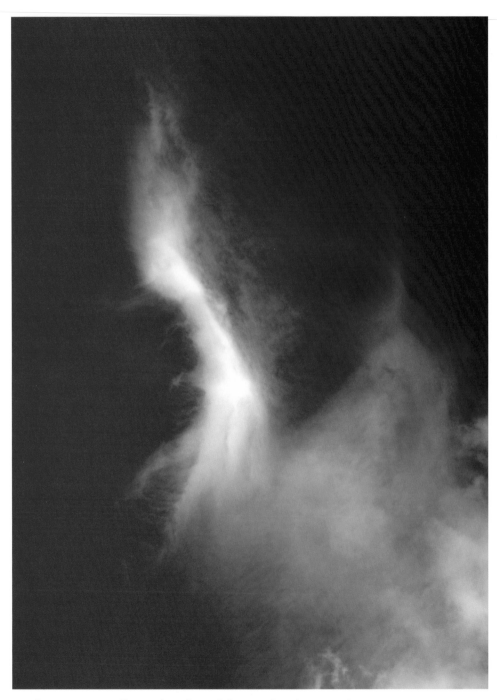

Meditation: Use all your hands and feet to do what is right.

Meditation: Follow the Light of the angelic realms and it will power you to great heights.

Meditation: Use your angelic self to care for your family and all others in need – everything deserves love.

Meditation: Follow me and don't let the sands of time slip away before you achieve your soul purpose.

Meditation: Be in balance in all aspects of your physical life and spiritual well-being.

Meditation: Be in appreciation of all those that support you unconditionally.

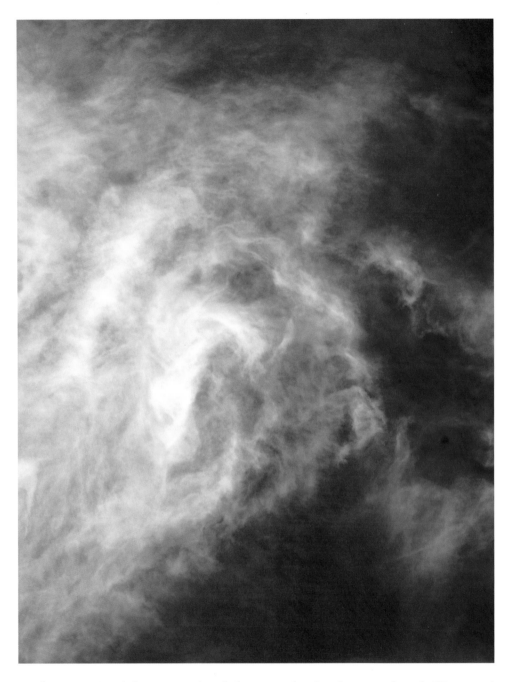

Meditation: Don't hang your head downward – Look upward with Hope and Confidence.

Meditation: Offer your love and kindness to others.

Meditation: Don't make yourself dizzy with the drama of others – focus on your angelic path.

Meditation: Be confident in your spiritual journey.

Meditation: Follow your dreams.

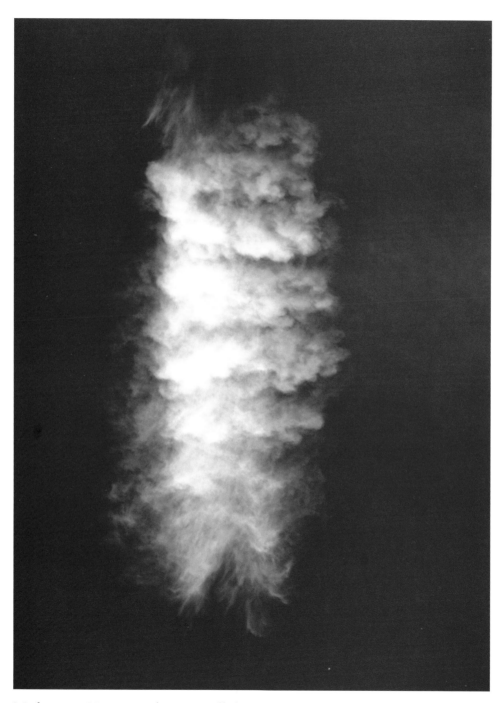

Meditation: Your inner beauty is all that matters.

Meditation: Be a feather in the winds of angelic energy and you will find your purpose.

Meditation: Sometimes you must let your ego follow and sometimes you must lead fearlessly.

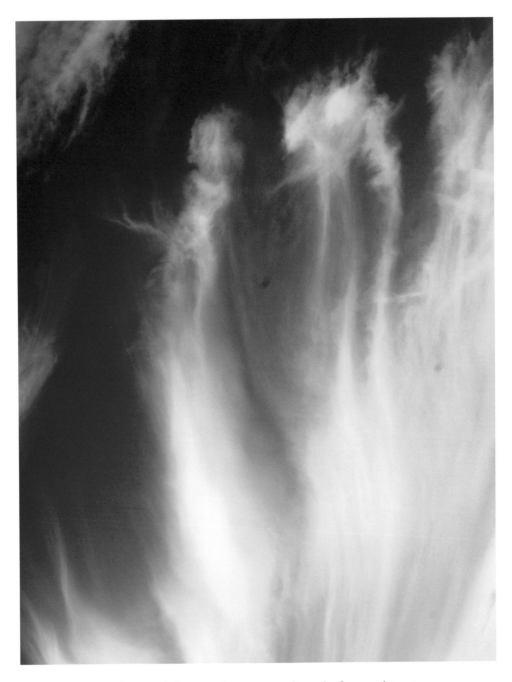

Meditation: Analyze and discern the surroundings before making important decisions.

Meditation: Just be happy in who you are.

Meditation: Spread your Love and Compassion like the wind.

Meditation: Sometimes Love comes in couples and togetherness.

Meditation: Don't show your fear in your face – Show strength and courage.

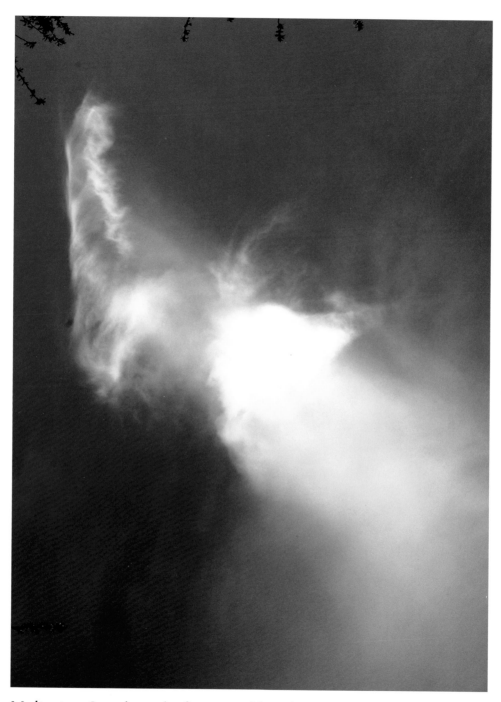

Meditation: Stay above the fray created by others...it only weakens you to get involved.

Meditation: Stand your ground confidently when following your spiritual path.

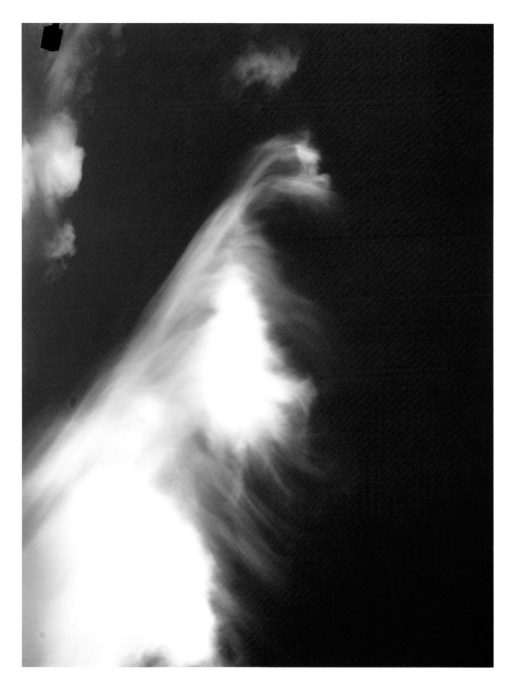

Meditation: Have your antennae up and working when seeking truth from lies – Discern.

Meditation: Don't be surprised when angel messages come your way – it is about using your abilities of communication and listening.

Meditation: Dance along with your angels and put nothing but positive thoughts into your mind and spirit.

Meditation: There are no limits when you embrace the angelic within you.

Meditation: Have nothing but fun as you incorporate your inner child within you.

Meditation: Look within yourself for the answers. Consult your higher self.

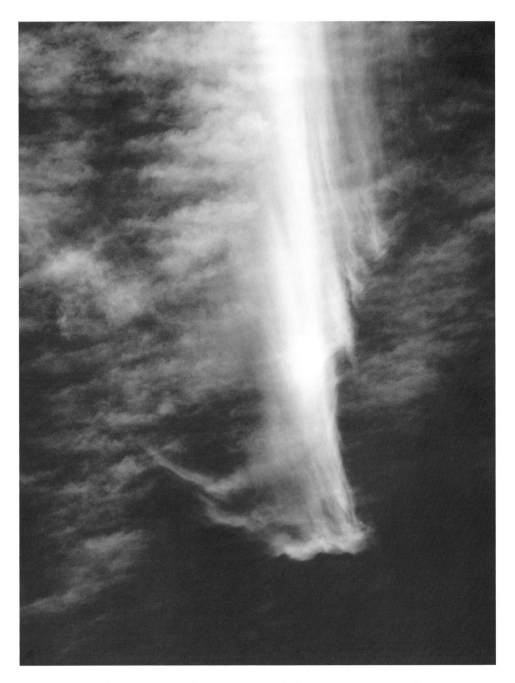

Meditation: Clearly you need to stay grounded when you are traveling your spiritual path.

Meditation: Learn the lessons of patience and persistence.

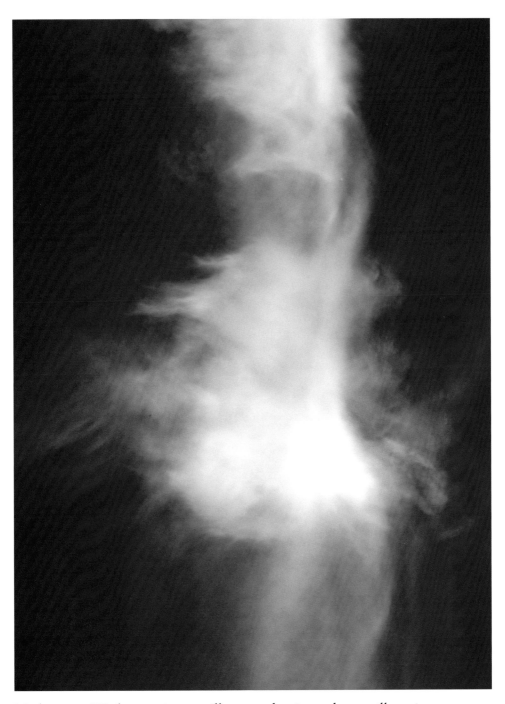

Meditation: Work in patience, stillness, and quiet and you will receive.

Meditation: Always survey where you are before making big decisions.

Meditation: With your angelic abilities, you can reach for the stars.

Meditation: To achieve your goals, you should consider patience, compassion, and kindness.

Meditation: You have free will to make your choice and decisions in this life.

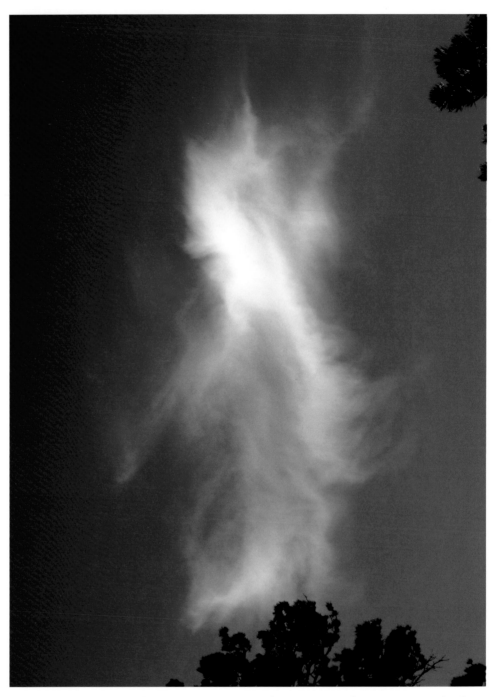

Meditation: Negativity can never win over the person with a positive outlook.

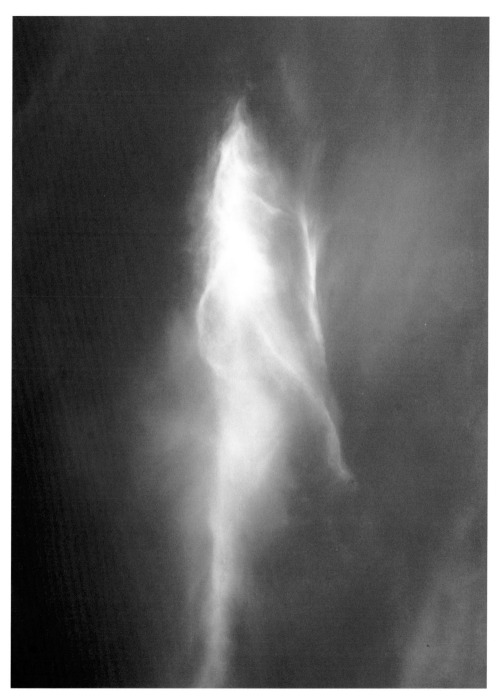

Meditation: Be strong, be wise, be compassionate, be caring.

Meditation: You may be surprised by the events you experience as you travel your path.

Meditation: Always carry yourself with confidence and wisdom.

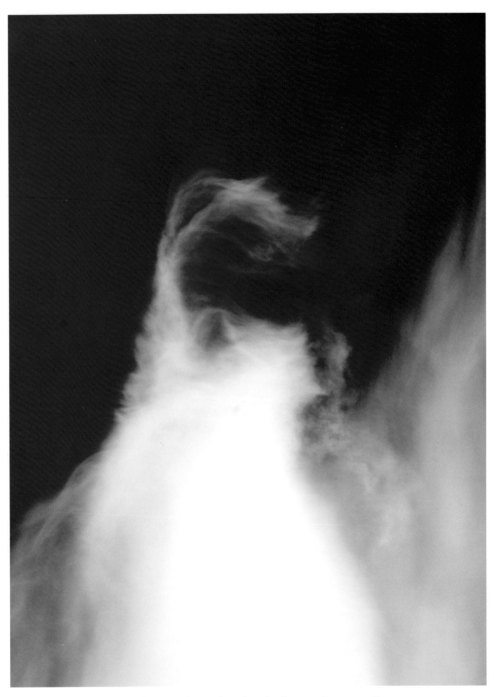

Meditation: Look to the angels in the clouds for guidance and support.

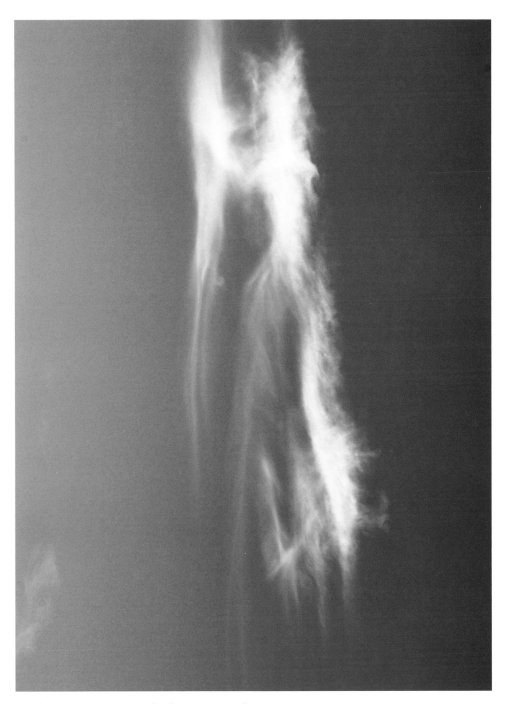

Meditation: Dance with the ones you love.

Meditation: Keep your mind, spirit, and body in balance.

Meditation: Seek to always be in a state of Joy.

Meditation: Be Respectful of others.

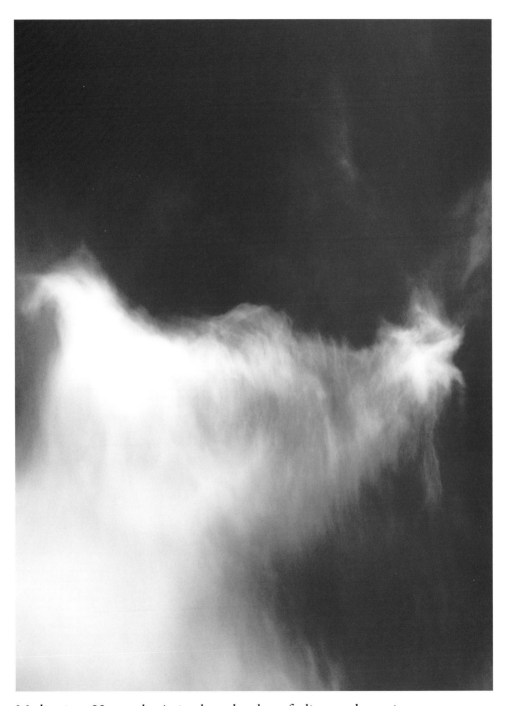

Meditation: Honor the Animals as they have feelings and emotions too.

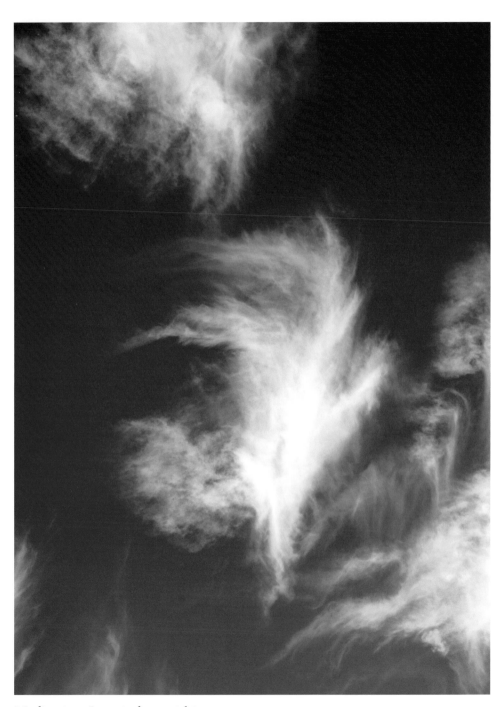

Meditation: Love is deep within you.

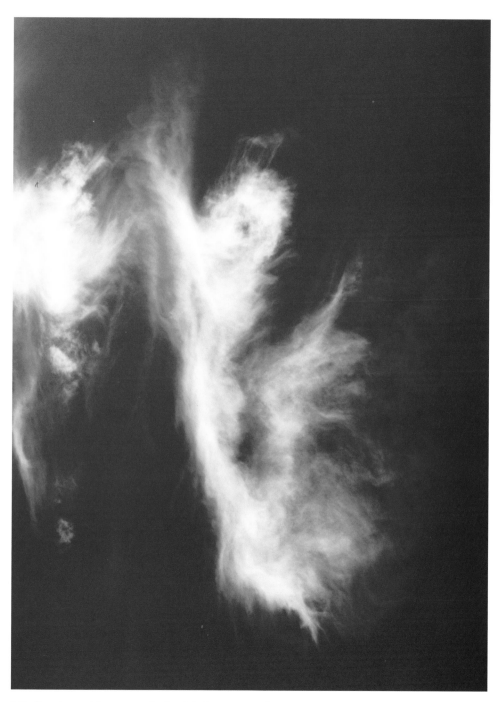

Meditation: Always seek the higher ground.

Meditation: Always be on the lookout – like the Meerkat – for any evil approaching you – protect yourself.

Meditation: Honor and Respect all of us that come in different forms, colors, and shapes.

Meditation: Be a model for expressing Love to all children.

Meditation: Follow the guidance of your angels and guides so that you may find the Love and Peace that is already within you.

Meditation: Seek the Truth in all things you encounter.

Meditation: There might be a time when you will have to be tough to protect yourself and the pursuit of your spiritual journey.

Meditation: There are times to be bold and determined.

Meditation: Don't let anyone else define you.

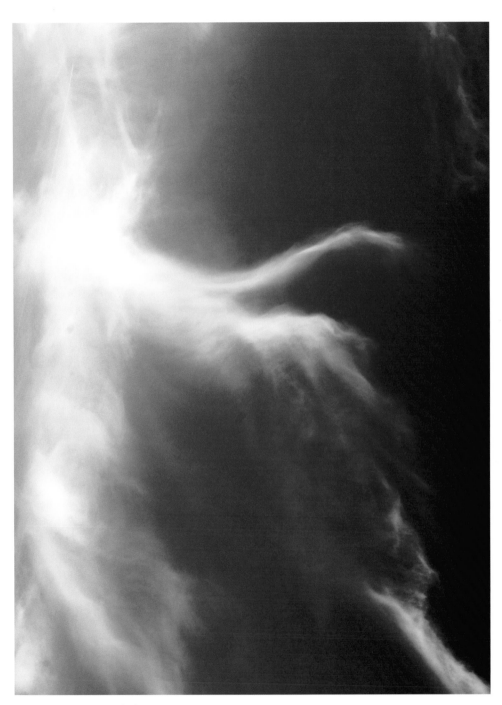

Meditation: Search for your answers.

Meditation: Always assess the landscape around you so that you make the best decisions for you.

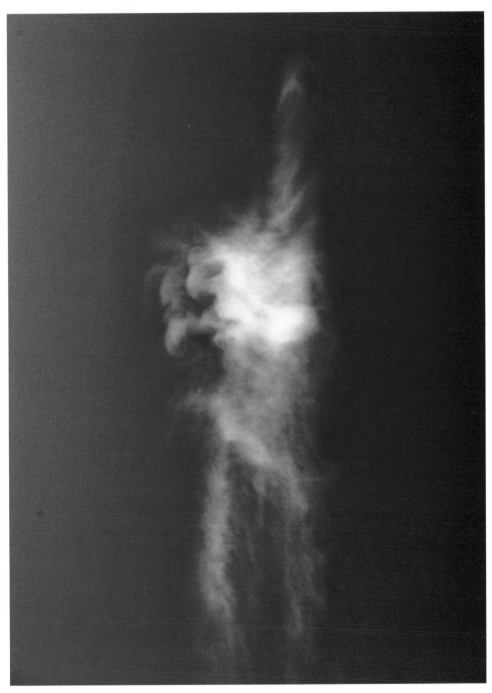

Meditation: Be wary of others as their agenda might be destructive to you.

Meditation: Be faithful to yourself and your angelic values.

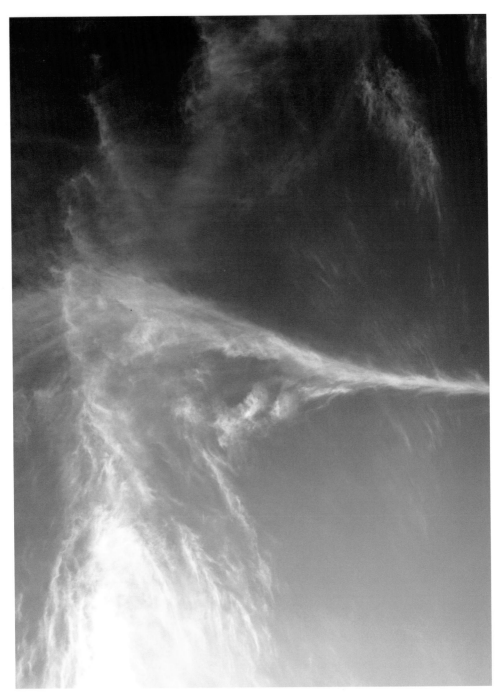

Meditation: Fly like the Hummingbird in joy, happiness, and love.

Meditation: Stay connected every day to the ones your love – every day – don't be shy to say I LOVE YOU to those you care about.

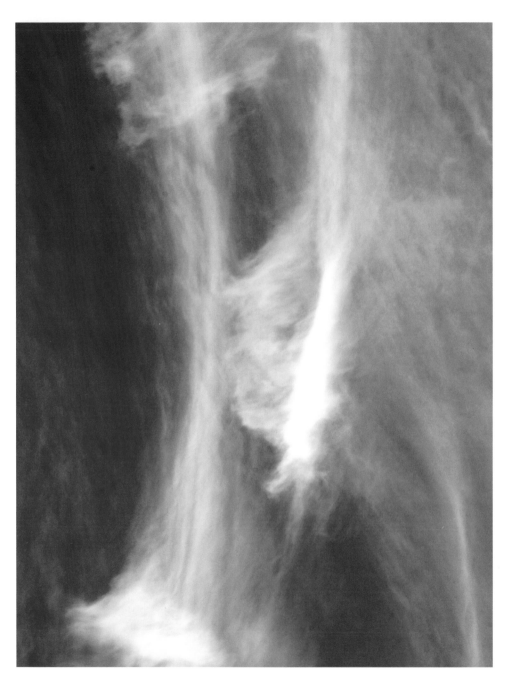

Meditation: Don't be afraid to speak your mind when it comes to what you need for your journey.

Meditation: Honor your Sacred Journey and protect yourself from others that may try to stop you.

Meditation: Sit down, relax, and detach yourself from this third dimensional world so that you can meditate clearly.

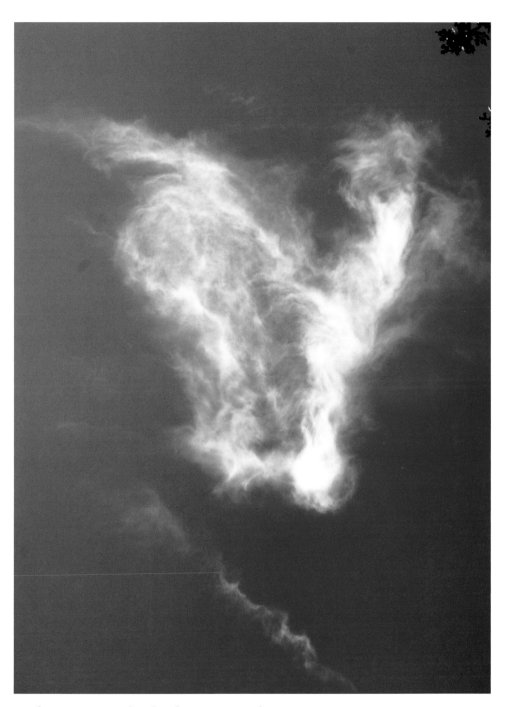

Meditation: Never be shy about Love and Caring.

Meditation: Allow others to feel your happiness and confidence by always expressing a smile.

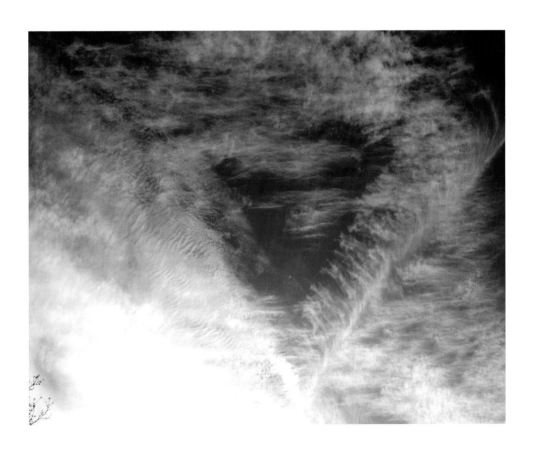

Meditation: Visualize the Triangle of Protection of your spiritual self.

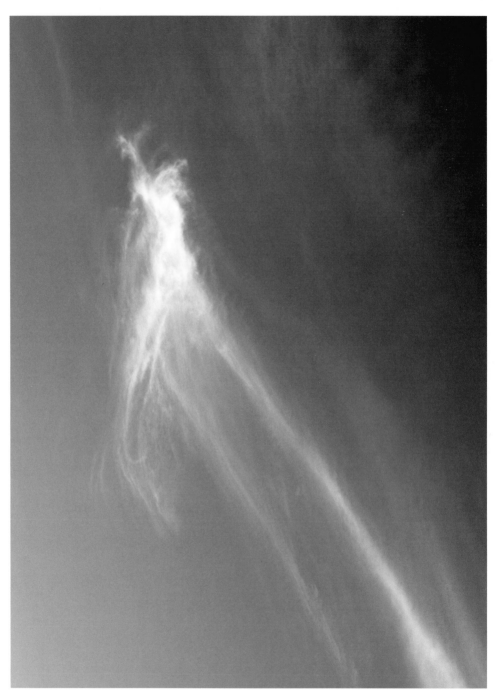

Meditation: Don't let anyone stop you from flying as high as you want.

Meditation: Meditate on the magical nature of the fairy so that you may use these talents to be of service to others.

Meditation: Violence is not necessary. Just show your powerful nature when confronted with evil.

Meditation: Be courageous and decisive so that you may lead rather than follow others.

Meditation: Don't pout and throw a tantrum just because you did not get your way. You can't win every battle, so choose your issues carefully.

Meditation: Saying nothing sometimes is better than arguing. Let others talk first, honor their opinions, then speak your mind.

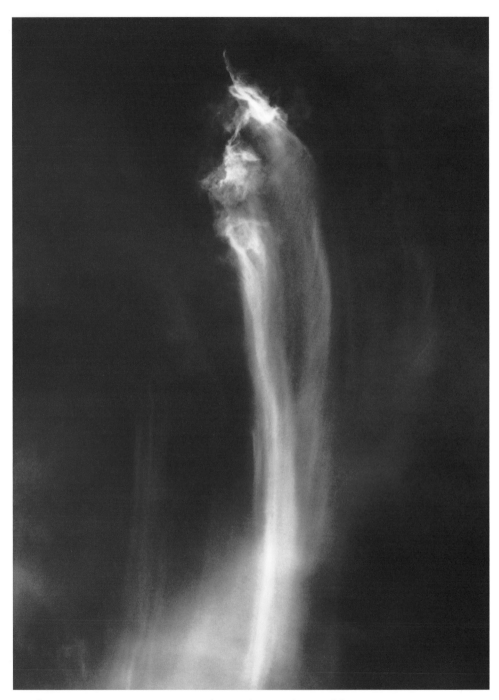

Meditation: One person, one soul can change the world.

Meditation: Don't put your arms up in disgust. Be calm and patient and plan your strategy to achieve your goals.

Meditation: Be expansive in your outlook on your life and spiritual path.

Meditation: Be focused, deliberate, and patient like the Tiger and you will be rewarded.

Meditation: With the lion comes courage and dignity. Use these qualities well.

Meditation: You have the skills of a seasoned pilot – focused and deliberate.
Let yourself fly solo.

Meditation: When you have a tough decision to make, allow your Heart to assist you in the answer.

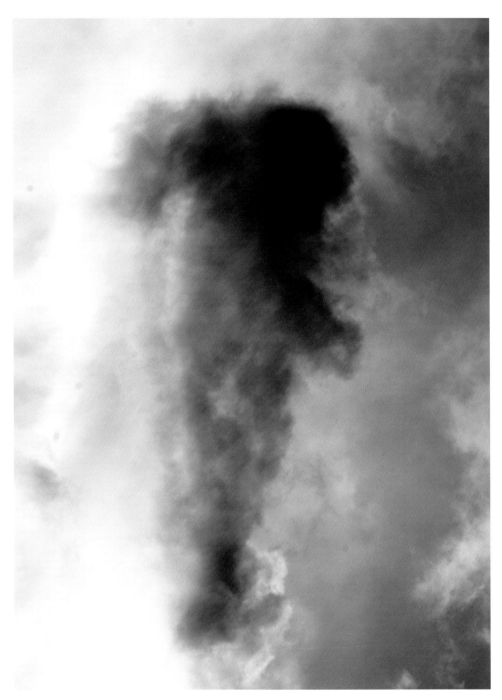

Meditation: Black and White are both beautiful.

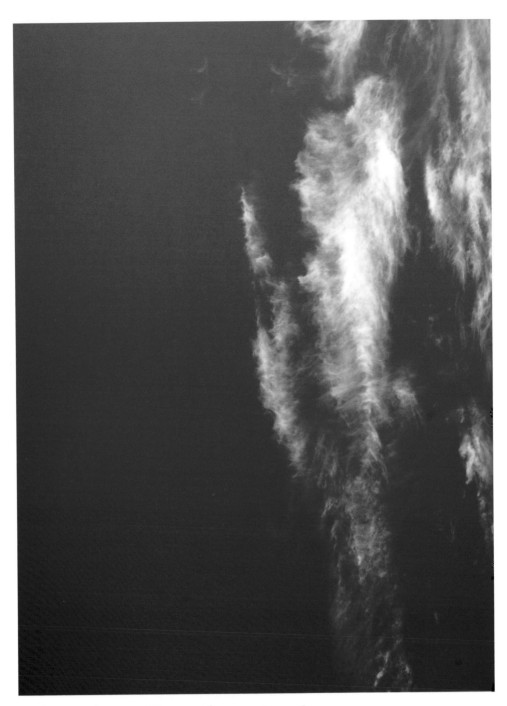

Meditation: Let your Heart guide you to Inner Peace.

Meditation: If you don't have all the answers, seek help or do your research – don't guess.

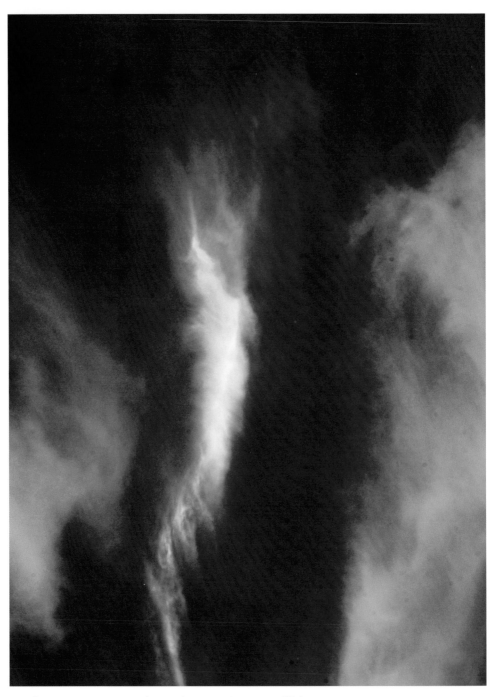

Meditation: You are a divine being – let youself shine.

Meditation: Be the glory that is within you.

Meditation: You are a person of many faces. Remove that mask that shields you so you can show that spiritual being within you.

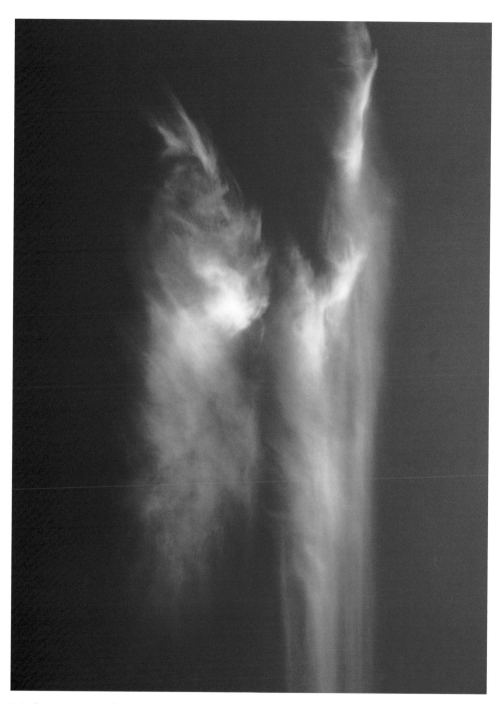

Meditation: Work together with others and show your leadership qualities.

Meditation: You may need help from others as you take your journey – be kind, listen to their views, and make them feel very important.

Meditation: You must learn to laugh at yourself. It is a great quality of human beings.

Meditation: Perhaps you should volunteer your talents to a person or group that needs help – be a loyal servant.

Meditation: You can still be very important without all that ego.

Meditation: Show your appreciation and gratitude for your life in this world at this time in history.

Meditation: Let your being, your energy, your goodness touch as many others as you can.

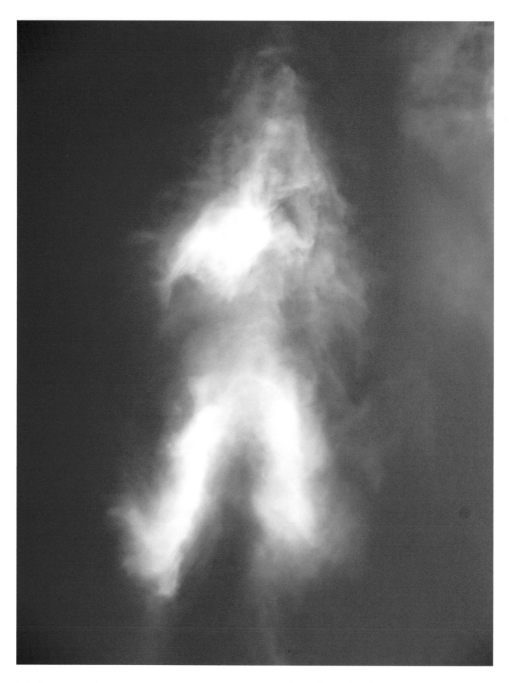

Meditation: Respect your Divine intuition – don't be afraid to walk the path shown by your intuition.

Meditation: Each day, take the time to do something good or of value for someone else.

Meditation: Sometimes it is important to recognize that you should stay at home and relax. Let the Divine energies time to come to you.

Meditation: Abundance comes in many forms. Allow yourself to work for and receive your abundance.

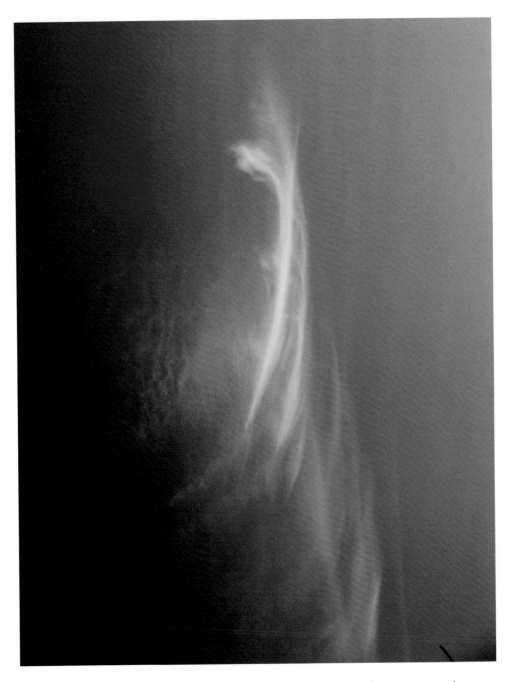

Meditation: Make yourself available each day for a period of prayer or meditation even if it is just a few minutes.

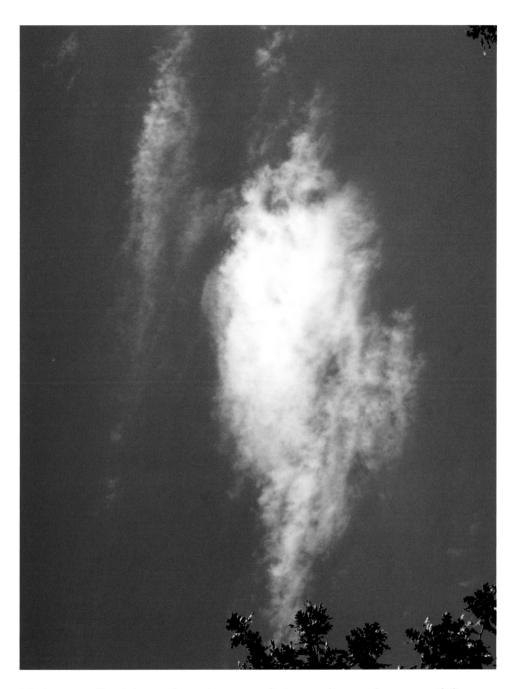

Meditation: Don't be a taker – it is not a divine quality – take responsibility for yourself.

Meditation: Don't wander aimlessly through life. Make a plan to alter your situation. Create a productive life helping others. That is the divine path.

Meditation: Bring happiness and joy to other people in your family, business, and others you might meet.

Meditation: Be aware of any persons exhibiting deceit and lies around you. They may not be good for you.

Meditation: Seek inspiration from others you meet. Allow yourself to inspire others as well.

Meditation: Work together in harmony with others as a team.

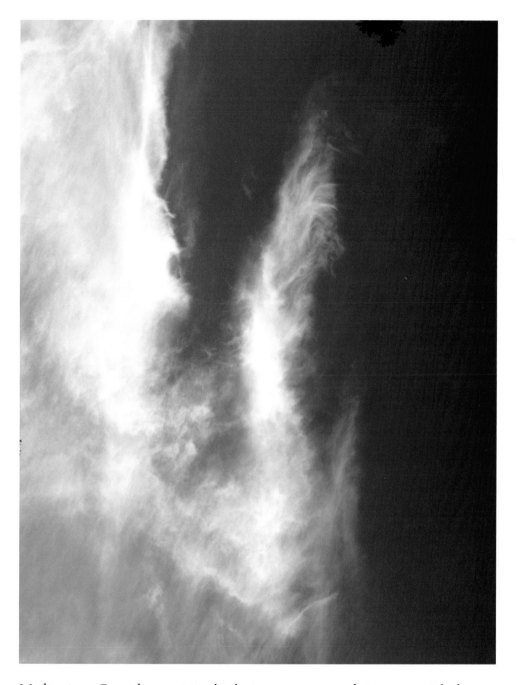

Meditation: Consider a spiritual pilgrimage to a sacred site or special place so that you may enhance your spiritual qualities and self.

Meditation: Be aware that some issues you encounter may have more than two sides.

Meditation: Despite our human need to see immediate action and reward your spiritual path works differently – focus on Patience, Patience, Patience.

Meditation: Follow the magic that is within you and it will serve you well.

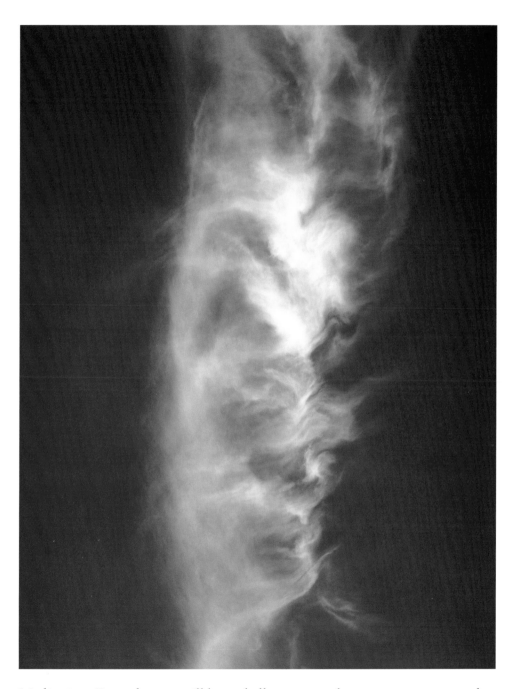

Meditation: Every day you will have challenges so make sure you are prepared to meet and overcome them.

Meditation: Trust all of your five physical senses. They are key to your determination if something might be bad for you.

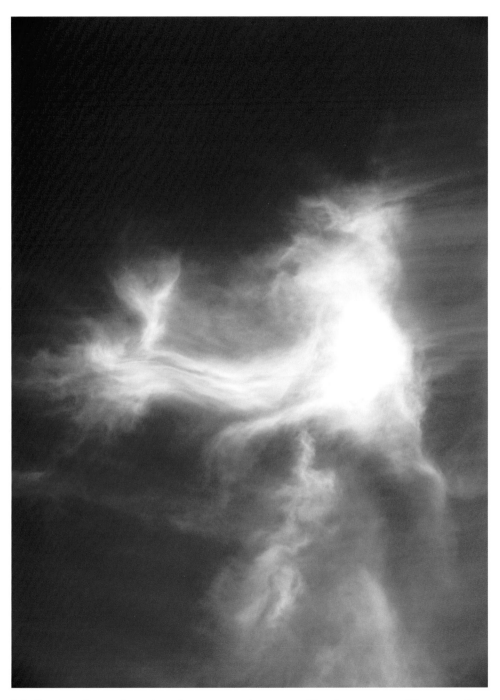

Meditation: It may be a time for you to enjoy yourself and treat yourself to some fun.

Meditation: New opportunities and ideas might be emerging soon so be open to the possibilities.

Meditation: Nuture yourself with healthy food and drink, beautiful surroundings, and people with positive energies.

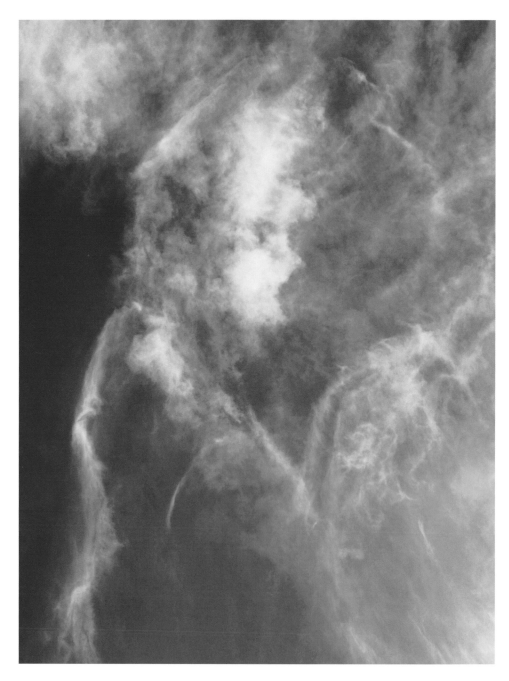

Meditation: The Goddess affirms that you have the ability to heal yourself and others just by allowing yourself to grow into your divine self.

Meditation: It is important to embrace the power of your Heart – the love, the caring, and the compassion. Make decisions using your Heart.

Meditation: Don't set limits on yourself and your abilities – you can achieve all that you desire.

Meditation: Let the Sun empower you, energize you, and guide you on your spiritual journey each day.

List of Meditations

"Celebrate Life with Love and Gratitude"

Carol and Tom hope you have enjoyed *Simply Angelic*. We have had fun bringing all of these angelic messages and photographs to you. Our simple message is that there is only LOVE! Each of us has the ability to LOVE and bring LOVE to others. There is not a better gift to give yourself and others.

With LOVE,

Carol   *Tom*

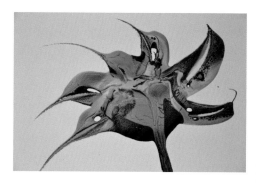

Tom Lumbrazo is also a fine artist!
You can see more examples
of Tom's art at his website
www.whenangelstouch.com

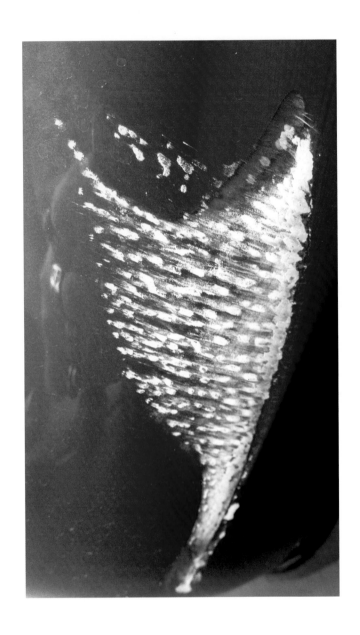

Final Meditation: Aways allow an angel to protect your backside ☺

You can order copies of this book *Simply Angelic*,
or Tom and Carol's previous books
Journey to the Clouds, and *Faces of the Universe*
through Tom's website at www.whenangelstouch.com
or by emailing him at Tom@whenangelstouch.com
or by phone at 916.782.8408

You can order prints of the photos in this book
from 8" by 10" to 30" by 40"
by emailing Tom at Tom@whenangelstouch.com

Prints can be mounted and also can be framed.
Prices will be determined at the time of order.

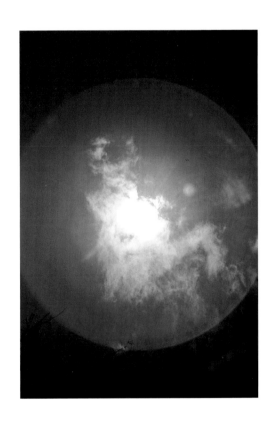

make peace